Old English Meter and
Linguistic Theory

Old English Meter and Linguistic Theory

GEOFFREY RUSSOM

Department of English
Brown University

CAMBRIDGE UNIVERSITY PRESS

Cambridge

London   New York   New Rochelle

Melbourne   Sydney

Published by the Press Syndicate of the University of Cambridge
The Pitt Building, Trumpington Street, Cambridge CB2 1RP
32 East 57th Street, New York, NY 10022, USA
10 Stamford Road, Oakleigh, Melbourne 3166, Australia

First published 1987

Printed in the United States of America

Library of Congress Cataloging-in-Publication Data
Russom, Geoffrey.
Old English meter and linguistic theory.
Bibliography: p.
Includes index.
1. English language – Old English, ca. 450–1100 –
Versification.   2. Beowulf – Versification.
3. Versification.   I. Title.
PE257.R87   1987   429'.16   86-34323
ISBN 0 521 33168 4

British Library Cataloging-in-Publication data applied for.

CONTENTS

Contents

Contents

Contents

PREFACE

A theorist confronted with an ancient meter like that employed in *Beowulf* begins work by attempting to identify the normative verse pattern. The next step is to identify legitimate deviations from the norm. A common type of deviation is often characterized as an "allowable exception" (see Halle and Keyser 1971, 165–6, for a recent discussion of this term). In the case of a poem such as *Beowulf* it is no easy matter to identify the normative pattern or the "allowable exceptions." We owe much to the painstaking statistical analyses of Sievers and Bliss, which have isolated problematic verses for further investigation. Yet some important questions remain unanswered. Why does the poet deviate from the norm in some respects while refusing, with remarkable persistence, to deviate in other respects? Why are some types of deviation so much more common than others? Why should a meter of this kind arise in a Germanic language? As we search for answers to such questions, we can turn for assistance to several specialized fields of study. Paleography and textual criticism can help us refine the corpus of examples to be explained. Philology and theoretical linguistics can enhance our understanding of the poet's complex artistic medium, the Old English language. Studies of other metrical systems may provide useful models. In this book I argue that advances in several fields now make it possible to provide a coherent rule system for Old English poetry, a system that defines the norm and explains the limits of deviation. Although I employ a variety of methodologies, I have tried wherever possible to work from first principles, without presupposing knowledge usually restricted to specialists in a single field.

Preface

Bliss (1958, vi) remarks that the frequent necessity for cross-reference made it impossible to publish his work in a series of articles. I have faced the same problem. Each rule presented below is justified to some extent on independent grounds, but in order to justify the theory as a whole I must show that the rules interact with one another properly. In this situation I have been fortunate to receive advice from scholars who saw preliminary versions of the argument. Thanks go first of all to Paul Kiparsky, whose work in metrics and phonology did much to inspire this project. As a result of his constructive criticism, several rules have been revised. I also received help from scholars whose views on Old English meter differ from my own. S. J. Keyser found time in his busy schedule to spend several hours beside me at an MIT blackboard. The present organization of the book testifies in many ways to his advice. Thomas Cable heard a partial sketch of the theory presented in a seminar on Old English meter at the Medieval Institute (Russom 1984). He made useful suggestions about matters of notation, both in conversation and in subsequent correspondence. To a fellow participant in the seminar, Edwin Duncan, I am grateful for much stimulating discussion, especially on the subject of poetic compounds.

I have a special debt to former students James Spamer and Steven Guthrie, who took an interest in this project during its formative years. As always, Jacqueline Haring Russom has helped me with linguistic and editorial matters.

I have not attempted here to provide a history of previous research on Old English meter or to attack other metrists wherever I differ with them. To criticize a metrist's treatment of a given issue fairly, one must usually take into account the theoretical motivation for that treatment. Meaningful evaluation of all rival theories would have made the book far too long. Critical commentary is directed primarily toward the common reference point for all who study Old English meter, the theory of Sievers (1885, 1893). It has seemed most important to explain my own ideas as clearly as possible, and to acknowledge the influence of the many previous researchers whose results I incorporate.

0

INTRODUCTION

0.1 Preliminary Observations

Those who study Old English poetry seldom disagree about certain of its fundamental properties. Thanks in part to the punctuation of the scribes,[1] a theorist can isolate two significant metrical domains, the *verse* or *half-line* and the *line*. Metrical constraints operate within each domain, allowing for some grammatical combinations of words while ruling out others. We find, for example, many verses like *furþur fēran* "to go farther" (254a),[2] consisting of two words with the common Old English trochaic pattern of a long stressed syllable followed by an unstressed syllable.[3] On the other hand, the more than six thousand verses of *Beowulf* include none like *tryddodon tīrfæste* "the glorious ones advanced," where each word has a long stressed syllable followed by two syllables of lesser stress. The absence of this type is particularly significant because we do find verses like *tryddode tīrfæst* "the glorious one advanced" (922a). By avoiding certain inflected forms of phrases otherwise acceptable as half-lines, the poet betrays an awareness of strict metrical rules. At the level of the line we detect rules that require placement of alliterating syllables in certain positions. In a line consisting of four fully stressed words,[4] for example, the first word alliterates obligatorily with the third and the last must not alliterate.

Sievers and others have provided detailed arguments showing that the poet avoided a number of imaginable verse patterns.[5] At present, however, no single set of rules distinguishing metrical patterns from unmetrical patterns has achieved consensus. The current lack of generalized metrical criteria makes it difficult to

I

deal with the question of complexity. Some of the more complex patterns have a very low relative frequency, but occur too often to ignore. Other patterns occur so seldom that they could well result from scribal error; but they might also represent types just slightly more complex than the rare patterns of undisputed status (cf. Bliss 1958, sections 84–7).

0.2 Theoretical Framework

In this book I employ four general principles to explain the metrical restrictions observed by the *Beowulf* poet:

Principle I: *Foot patterns* correspond to native Old English word patterns. The foot patterns most easily perceived are those that correspond to the most common word patterns.

Principle II: The *verse* consists of two feet. Foot patterns corresponding to unusual word patterns add to the complexity of verses in which they appear.

Principle III: *Alliterative patterns* correspond to Old English stress patterns. A metrical rule that mimics the Old English compound stress rule determines the location of alliterating syllables.

Principle IV: The *line* consists of two adjacent verses with an acceptable alliterative pattern.

Principles I–IV amount to a claim that many intricacies of Old English meter reduce to intricacies of language. I assume that the native speaker of Old English would have possessed, as part of an internalized grammar, one set of rules specifying the word patterns attested in the language and another set determining the position of stress in a word with a given pattern.[6] I also assume that a native speaker introduced to poetry in the normal way could identify metrical rules as analogues of linguistic rules already learned. Once the native speaker grasped the relation between language and general principles of verse construction, many corollaries that must be made explicit for a speaker of Modern English would have followed as a matter of course.

When we consider how principles I–IV might relate to Old English linguistic rules, and through them to actual verses, several questions arise at once. We need to determine, first, what counts as a "word" for the purposes of the meter. Principle I would have little meaning if some word patterns were excluded arbitrarily from consideration. The concept of "word pattern," however, will require some discussion. A plausible theory would certainly include a foot pattern for each type of stressed simplex word; but what about compounds or function words? In Chapter 1 we begin by addressing such questions.

The theory must also take into account the fact that Old English verses may contain more than two words. Consider the following:

(1) (a) gomban gyldan 11a
         tribute to-yield
         "to pay tribute"

    (b) torht getǣhte 313a
         bright he-indicated
         "he pointed out the bright object"

    (c) grim ond grǣdig 121a
         grim and greedy
         "grim and greedy"

    (d) (ge-)wāc æt wīge 2629a
         failed in combat
         "failed in combat"

In Sievers (1885, 1893), verses such as (1b-d) are assigned, I think correctly, to the type represented by (1a), which has two trochaic words. Stating this claim within the framework of principles I-IV, we can say that the word group *grim ond* in (1c) mimics the phonological pattern of trochaic words[7] like *gomban*. To support such a claim, we must explain why (1c) corresponds to the pattern of (1a) rather than to that of (1b), since (1b) also appears to consist of two words, if we judge by the editorial spacing. One can imagine assigning *torht* to the first foot of a two-word verse, with *getǣhte* as the second foot. Why not, then, regard *grim* as the first foot of (1c) on the assumption that *ond grǣdig* mimics the pattern of *getǣhte*? Moreover, if (1b) represents a variant of the pattern in (1a), we need to justify grouping the *ge-* prefix together with *torht* rather than with *-tǣhte*. Finally, we must justify exclusion of *ge-*

from consideration in (1d). According to Sievers, this instance of the prefix stands in "anacrusis" as an extrametrical syllable.

If the Old English audience could recognize verses like (1b-d) as variants of the (1a) pattern, it must have internalized general procedures, applicable to all verses, for identifying extrametrical syllables and for determining which foot contained a given syllable included in the metrical pattern. Rules given in Chapter 1 attempt to represent these procedures explicitly.

Chapter 2 provides the rules that distinguish verse patterns reliably attested in *Beowulf* from other patterns that the poet rejects. These rules all follow from the general principle that feet corresponding to unusual word patterns add to the complexity of verse patterns. Chapters 3–6 apply the rules developed in the first two chapters to long-standing problems of Old English meter. In Chapter 3, I analyze a number of peculiar verses with extrametrical syllables. In Chapter 4, I consider the metrical interpretation of words with a complex or ambiguous phonological makeup. Chapter 5 relates some well-known anomalies in the relative frequency of verse patterns to the problems posed by very large and very small feet. Chapter 6 demonstrates that the rules proposed for normal verses also help to explain the so-called "hypermetrical verses."

Discussion of alliterative patterns begins in Chapter 7. Here I introduce two explicit rules as corollaries to principle III. A metrical subordination rule (47) determines the relative prominence of positions within the metrical pattern. A second rule (50) assigns alliterating syllables to the most prominent positions. Principle III may seem exotic at first glance, but it follows naturally, I think, from well-known facts about alliterative meters. Sievers (1893, section 22) pointed out that the constituents most frequently selected for alliteration are those with prominent phrasal stress. As Kuryłowicz (1970, 19) observed, this implies metrical subordination of strongly stressed constituents that do *not* alliterate. Chapter 8 deals with special peculiarities of "heavy verses" containing three or more prominently stressed words. In Chapter 9, the alliterative rules are used to investigate syntactic structures with problematic stress patterns.

The theory proposed here isolates a handful of exceptional verses in the *Beowulf* manuscript. Chapter 10 reviews previous discussion of these anomalies, which are often emended by editors. A few apparent exceptions yield to reanalysis, and the others seem to result from familiar types of scribal error. The chapter concludes with a demonstration of the way in which the theory distinguishes Old English poetry from Old English prose.

Chapter 11 provides a review of results obtained in previous chapters. Here I contend that the modest number of complexities in the theory reflect intrinsic complexities of poetic craft.

0.3 Acoustic Prominence and Metrical Significance

Although principles I-IV allow for incorporation of much previous scholarship, they are totally incompatible with the familiar claim that Old English half-lines consist of two main stresses and an indeterminate number of weaker stresses.[8] The emphasis on stressed syllables has, admittedly, a certain appeal. Confronted with a bewildering variety of phonological patterns in the poetry of a dead culture, it is natural to seize on the most salient linguistic features. The two-stress theory has a special attraction for those who believe that verse is in a very strict sense "for the ear," that its rules govern prominent acoustic features of spoken language like changes in volume or measurable pauses.[9] However, the metrists most closely concerned with *Beowulf* have usually rejected this approach, because it fails to provide for constraints on the positioning of unstressed syllables.[10] When we formulate methodological criteria, moreover, we ought to reflect that Old English poetry was not designed for speakers of other languages, but for native speakers of Old English, who were aware of many linguistic features with no prominent acoustic correlates.

The theory proposed here will make crucial reference to one such feature: the word boundary. Although the word boundary does not correspond to a measurable pause in connected discourse, it plays an important role in linguistic processes, and for that reason appears in the abstract word patterns employed by phonological theory.[11] If foot patterns correspond to linguistic word patterns, as principle I asserts, we should expect to find metrically significant foot boundaries analogous to the boundaries of words. In insisting on the importance of word boundaries, I do not claim originality. The 1938 study of Mácha by Jakobson employs a concept of the foot much like that advocated here (see Jakobson 1979, 433–85). Jakobson asserts, for example, that the linguistic prototype for the Czech trochee is the normative trochaic word of the Czech language (p. 438 and passim). To distinguish their innovative iambic meters from the traditional trochaic meters, Czech poets like Mácha align word boundaries with the boundaries of iambic feet so persistently that the intended grouping of syllables becomes obvious to the audience (see especially p. 454, note 39). A similar concept of "word foot" is employed by Travis (1973, 1–14) in his analysis of some Old Irish poems. These poems exhibit half-lines of two feet bound into lines of four feet by alliteration, and their meter has often been compared to the meter of *Beowulf*.

Kiparsky (1977) introduces some terms which I shall employ below. For Kiparsky, the foot is an ordered set of abstract metrical positions flanked by boundaries analogous to the boundaries of linguistic constituents. The trochaic foot might be represented as [S W], where the S or "strong" position normally corresponds to a stressed syllable, the W or "weak" position normally corresponds to an unstressed syllable, and the "brackets" ([,]) normally correspond to linguistic boundaries. When an unstressed syllable occupies an S position, or when a stressed syllable occupies a W position, what Kiparsky calls a *labeling mismatch* occurs. Failure to align boundaries in linguistic material with the boundaries of feet causes *bracketing mismatches*. Not all of the analytical procedures employed in Kiparsky (1977), which deals with meters of the Modern English period, are applicable to *Beowulf*. My concept of the metrical foot must be somewhat less abstract than Kiparsky's; and several types of mismatch that figure prominently in Kiparsky's discussion simply do not occur in Old English verse.[12] On the other hand, Old English materials provide straightforward evidence for certain claims about the significance of bracketing that are much more difficult to validate in the later period (cf. Kiparsky 1977, 223–235).

0.4 Meter and Rhythm

In what follows I will be concerned primarily with linguistic properties of reliably attested verse patterns rather than with musical rhythm. However, my findings seem quite compatible with the rhythmical interpretations of Pope (1942) and Creed (1966). Pope's controversial reanalysis of types B and C, which was motivated by rhythmical considerations, receives support of a purely linguistic character in section 1.5.2 below. Moreover, the central role played by the trochaic word, as defined in section 2.5, suggests a trochaic rhythmical norm like that of later Western music. Pope's use of present-day musical notation seems to me quite compatible with the linguistic structure of Old English metrical texts.

1

THE FOOT

1.1 Words

All speakers have "a feeling for what is, or is not, a word" (Bauer 1983, section 2.2, p. 8). Providing a formal definition of "word" for a given language can be a difficult task, however (cf. Jespersen 1924, 92–5). Several types of pertinent evidence exist for Old English, but these sometimes give conflicting testimony.

1.1.1 Unstressed Prefixes

Consider the familiar idea that the "word" is an inseparable syntactic constituent. Old English *gesēon* "see" and *behealdan* "hold" qualify as words by this criterion because no other constituent can intervene between their prefixes *(ge-, be-)* and their verbal roots. The close association between prefix and root during the Old English period was a relatively recent development, however. Gothic testifies to an earlier state of the Germanic languages during which prefixes acted more like function words. At this point, we find constructions such as *ga u ƕa sēƕi* "if he were seeing anything," where a form of *ga-saíƕan,* the cognate of *gesēon,* has its "prefix" split from the root by *u* "if" and *ƕa* "anything" (see Meid 1967, sections 42–55). The Gothic evidence tallies with the simplest formulation of the Germanic stress shift rule, which states that stress shifted to the first syllable of all accented words. If Germanic speakers had regarded verbal prefixes as part of the word, such prefixes would have acquired stress; yet they did not. The same prefixal elements behave very differently when compounded with nouns and adjectives. In *bīspell* "proverb," for ex-

ample, the spelling *bī-* indicates stress on the prefix, in contrast to
the unstressed form *be-* of *behealdan* (see OEG, section 73). It
seems clear that a nominal or adjectival prefix was regarded as
part of a compound word during the Germanic stress shift, but
that the verbal prefix was regarded as a function word.[1]

Certain Old English phonological rules show that the earlier
feeling for the "word" persisted into the period when verbal prefixes could no longer be split from the following verbal stem. One
such rule deletes the voiceless fricative spelled *h* between vowels or
between a vowel and a voiced consonant (see OEG, sections 461–
6). A stem-final *h* appears in *hēah* "high," but not in the weak
inflected form *hēan,* derived from an underlying **hēahan,* where
the stem-final *h* stands between vowels. Forms like *behealdan*
show that this rule does not apply when the first vowel lies within
a prefix. In *behealdan,* the *h* counts as word-initial, and the prefix
be- has a status like that of a preposition. If we assume that Old
English phonology defines unstressed prefixes as function words,
we can simply state that *h* disappears between voiced sounds at
the level of the word.[2]

1.1.2 Compound Formations

Compounds and words with stressed prefixes have a somewhat
ambiguous status with respect to rules of word-level phonology such
as h-loss. These rules apply as usual in familiar forms with a long
history such as *bīot* "a promise," derived from an earlier *bī-hāt.* In
neologisms or in less frequently used formations of the same type,
however, *h* remains (cf. *ǣ-hiwness* "lack of color"). *Bīot* and *ǣ-hiw-
ness* represent opposite points of a gradual process that all compounds can undergo if they attain general currency. Entering the
language with subordination of the stress on the secondary constituent, a compound behaves at first like two words in other respects.
After the feeling for the subordinated element as a separable constituent weakens, the whole compound may undergo word-level
rules that at first did not apply. Stress on the subordinated element
becomes further weakened and may be lost altogether (see OEG,
sections 87–92). The end result of this "lexicalization" process is a
large simplex word. The set of "compounds" employed by a given
speaker, then, is by no means homogeneous: Some will resemble two
words in most respects, while others will resemble simplexes.[3]

Morphological marking of Old English compounds often proves unreliable. An overt inflectional ending on the first of two constituents usually indicates a word group rather than a compound, although "genitive compounds" like *Hrefnawudu* "Ravens' Wood, Ravenswood" preserve their internal inflections. Sometimes it is difficult to distinguish an adjective without an overt inflectional ending from the first constituent of a compound. In Old English manuscripts, a string of constituents like *brād swurd* might be interpreted as "large sword" or as "broadsword." The scribes, who routinely separate the constituents of compounds by a word space, give us little help with such problems.

1.1.3 Function Words

We acknowledge the independent status of function words in many ways. The term "function word" itself implies that prepositions, conjunctions, articles, and other unstressed English lexical items have an integrity resembling that of major-category words (nouns, stressed verbs, and adjectives). Function words are often flanked by word spaces in spelling systems, and even those that undergo contraction with an adjacent stressed word must sometimes be regarded as independent "words" in certain respects (cf. Jespersen 1924, 94–5). On the other hand, words of minor category are much more likely to lose their independence than are words with prominent stress. In Bosworth-Toller, s.v. *dæg*, Old English *tō dæg* is represented as a two-word phrase. All modern English dictionaries agree in representing the descendant of this phrase, *today,* as a single word, since *to-* is no longer recognized as a separable constituent. The primarily grammatical role of function words also sets them apart from words of major category. Lightfoot (1982, 195–6) cites evidence from language pathology indicating that function words and major-category words are perceived in somewhat different ways. It seems, then, that unstressed function words are less "word-like" than are stressed lexical items with more prominent semantic content.

1.1.4 Summary

The issues raised in sections 1.1.1–1.1.3 suggest the following corollaries to Rule I:

The Foot

A. All stressed simplexes count as words.
B. Unstressed prefixes count as "function words."
C. A compound may count as one word or as two.
D. A "function word" may count as a word or as undefined linguistic material.

1.2 Word Patterns

In phonology, word-level rules apply not to individual words but to classes of words that exhibit the relevant structural properties. Principle I amounts to a claim that Old English foot patterns correspond to such natural word classes. Before we attempt a detailed discussion of foot patterns, we need to consider the concept of "word pattern" implicit in the phonology.

One striking characteristic of early Germanic languages is the strong expiratory stress that invests most of the articulative energy in the first part of the word, leaving the rest susceptible to reduction (OEG, section 331). Because short syllables require less energy than long syllables, an unaccented vowel following a short syllable is less prone to reduction than an unaccented vowel following a long syllable. In neuter a-stems, for example, the inflectional ending *-u* is lost after "long stems" like *wīf* "woman," *word* "word," but remains after "short stems" like *scip* "ship," with a short vowel followed by a single consonant. The phonological rule for vowel deletion would not distinguish among the sequences CVVC, CVCC, CVVCC, etc., where C stands for a consonant, single V stands for a short vowel, and double V stands for a long vowel. All these sequences are equivalent because they all trigger deletion of a following vowel, in contrast to the sequence CVC. Unstressed vowels also drop after the "resolvable" bisyllabic sequences CVCVC, CVCVCC, etc., consisting of a short stressed syllable followed by an unstressed syllable. Hence the neuter a-stem *werod* behaves like *wīf* and *word,* dropping the inflectional ending that remains in forms like *scipu*. The most important principle of phonological classification is that distinguishing long stressed syllables and resolvable sequences on the one hand from short stressed syllables on the other.

A second important feature of Germanic languages also involves stress and syllable length. Although short stressed monosyllables occur in some languages (e.g. Italian *no* "not" in *Credo di no* "I think not"), this situation does not arise in Old English. All Old English stressed monosyllables have either a long vowel or a syllable-final consonant (cf. Introduction, note 3). The smallest stressed words with short root syllables (e.g. *scipu, werod*) constitute resolvable sequences. In Old English, then, stress normally implies a phonological domain of one long syllable or two short syllables.

1.3 Derivation of Foot Patterns from Word Patterns

If Old English phonology equates resolvable sequences with long stressed syllables, we would expect to find the same equation in metrical patterns. Here I will assume that a single abstract metrical position, which I represent with a capital S, is derived from resolvable sequences as well as from long stressed syllables. An alternative way of stating this relation between language and meter is to say that resolvable sequences and long stressed syllables *generate* the same type of metrical S position. The idealized word patterns that we call feet will not contain metrical positions corresponding to short stressed syllables (cf. Kuryłowicz 1970, 9). Forms such as *wīf, word, werod,* and *scipu* will all generate feet consisting of a single S.

The salient feature of Old English compounds is subordination of stress on the root syllable in the second constituent. The abstract metrical position derived from a subordinated root syllable can be represented by a lower-case s. Resolvable sequences in subordinated constituents will generate a single s position.

Inflectional syllables of Old English words were unstressed, and underwent sound changes not characteristic of stressed syllables (see OEG, sections 330–97). I will use the notation x to indicate metrical positions derived from syllables of this type. The root syllables in certain Old English function words were also unstressed (e.g. *ond* "and," *oþþe* "or"). Feet derived from such function words will consist entirely of x positions. It is important to note that some unstressed Old English words consist of a single short syllable (e.g. *be* "by"). The possibility of resolution cannot arise with respect to unstressed syllables because they have no standard length. Every unstressed syllable, whether long or short, will therefore generate a metrical position. This means that an unstressed word like *ofer* "over," with a short root syllable, will generate the foot pattern xx. In discussion of extrametrical words below, I will employ the notation (x), (xx), etc., to indicate unstressed syllables lying outside the metrical pattern.[4]

The medial syllables in certain trisyllabic words had a reduced stress, distinct from secondary stress on the one hand and from zero stress on the other.[5] If we posited a fourth type of metrical position corresponding to syllables of reduced stress, the resulting system of contrasts would look quite unusual. Here I will assume that syllables of reduced stress generate x positions.[6] The resulting three-way distinction among S, s, and x resembles that observed in "compound" meters by Borroff (1962, 164–89).

1.4 A List of Allowable Foot Patterns

The metrical system includes the following foot patterns, derived from native Old English words according to the principles defined above:

Feet	Corresponding Words
x	ond ("and") ge- (prefix)
S	gōd ("good"), n. sg. fem.; tilu ("good"), n. sg. fem.
xx	oþþe ("or") ofer- (prefix)
Sx	dryhten ("lord") þolode ("he suffered")
Ss	sǣ-mann ("sea-man, sailor"); mægen-wudu ("power-wood, spear")
Sxx	bealdode ("he encouraged") gryrelicu ("terrible"), n. sg. fem.
Ssx	sǣ-mannes ("sailor's"), g. sg. sigor-ēadig ("blessed with victory")
Sxs	middan-geard ("middle earth") inwit-searo ("malicious cunning")
Sxxs	sibbe-ge-driht ("band of kinsmen")[7]

The list of corresponding words includes forms containing resolvable sequences (e.g. *tilu,* with short radical *i* followed by one consonant). Note that whereas unstressed prefixes count as function words, the unstressed infix of *sibbegedriht (-ge-)* counts as part of the compound.

The metrical system allows for a variety of foot patterns, but by no means for all imaginable patterns. We have x feet and xx feet, but there are no xxx feet because Old English has no trisyllabic unstressed words.[8] Since the first constituent of a compound will have an S or Sx pattern, and since the only unstressed infixes have a single syllable, as -ge- does, there can be no patterns such as Sxxxs, Sxxxxs, etc.[9] The definition of unstressed prefixes as function words eliminates all foot patterns with rising stress (xS, xxS, xxSx, etc.).

1.5 Word Groups within the Foot

In the simplest verses, each foot contains a single word; but the demands of epic storytelling make it impossible for the poet to realize the ideal two-word pattern in every verse.[10] Often the foot will contain a word group that mimics the structure of an individual word. To the extent that word groups deviate from the ideal pattern of a single word, they create *mismatches* (as defined in Kiparsky 1977, 196). Any mismatch adds to metrical complexity, and verses with certain combinations of mismatches will occur seldom or not at all. A poet who deviates from the ideal pattern in one respect will be especially careful to conform in other respects.

1.5.1 Labeling Mismatches

An important type of matching rule restricts the linguistic properties of actual syllables with respect to the "labeling" of abstract metrical positions (S, s, x). In the simplest case, the label on a metrical position gives an accurate representation of the type of linguistic material occupying that position. S positions, for example, are normally occupied by the type of linguistic material that generates S positions (long syllables with primary stress or corresponding resolvable sequences). A *labeling mismatch* occurs when the label does not give an accurate picture of the contents.

The following rules restrict labeling mismatches in Old English verse:

(2) (a)   A syllable with primary stress may occupy an S position or (under certain conditions) an s position.

(b)   A syllable with zero stress must occupy an x position.

(c)   A syllable with secondary stress may occupy an s position or (under certain conditions) an S position.[11]

These rules forbid certain types of labeling mismatches that occur
frequently in meters with a single foot pattern. In iambic pentameter, a syllable with zero stress can occupy a position normally
associated with a syllable of primary stress, and a syllable of secondary stress can occupy a position normally associated with a
syllable of zero stress (cf. Halle and Keyser 1971, 166). Neither
option exists in Old English poetry, which provides metrical variety through the employment of numerous foot patterns rather
than through deviation from a single pattern. Note that the labeling rules impose no restrictions on syllables with "reduced stress."
Since these syllables have no well-defined stress level, they evade
the restrictions in (2b-c), and may occupy any type of metrical
position.[12]

1.5.2 *Bracketing Mismatches*

It is well known that Old English half-lines correspond to natural
syntactic constituents with readily identifiable boundaries. We
can isolate verses with considerable confidence in part because
their boundaries correspond so well to linguistic boundaries (see
Introduction, note 1). Jakobson (1938) shows that poets also
tend to align prominent linguistic boundaries (notably word
boundaries) with the boundaries of metrical feet. Kiparsky uses
the term *bracketing mismatch* to describe a situation in which
the foot boundary does not correspond to a prominent linguistic
boundary.

I propose the following *bracketing rules* for Old English meter:

(3) (a)   Every foot boundary must coincide with a word boundary. Note: the internal boundaries of compounded
forms count as "word boundaries" for the purposes of
this rule.[13]

(b) In verses with three or more stressed words, the stressed words are assigned to feet in accordance with their syntactic constituency. Note: compounds count as two words for the purposes of this rule.[14]

Rules (3a-b) are motivated by fundamental principles of the theory proposed here. If feet correspond to words, it follows that foot boundaries should correspond to word boundaries. Moreover, when a verse contains three stressed words, it seems logical that the two stressed words assigned to the same foot should form a natural constituent. Consider the following verse, for example:

(4) brim / blōde fāh 1594a
the-sea with-blood stained
"the sea stained with blood"

Here three fully stressed words (nouns and adjectives) occur in a single verse, and the audience must determine which foot contains two words. In such cases, Sievers (1893, section 23.3) appeals to the concept of close syntactic composition. According to Sievers, the phrase *blōde fāh* qualifies as a foot because it forms a natural constituent (compare compound adjectives like *blōdfāh* "blood-stained"). The string of words *brim blōde,* on the other hand, does not form a natural constituent at any level of syntactic analysis.

Sievers's way of dividing verses like (4) is more than an arbitrary classification procedure. Syntactic criteria play a crucial role, for example, in determining the correct location of alliterating syllables. Consider the following:

(5) (a) *folm / blōde fāh
hand stained with blood
"hand stained with blood"

(b) fīf nihta / fyrst 545a
five nights' time
"for a period of five nights"

The second constituent of an Old English compound does not alliterate unless the first constituent alliterates also.[15] When an Sxs foot is occupied by a compound word like *middangeard,* alliteration will therefore occur on the S position occupied by the root syllable of the first constituent *(mid-)* rather than on the s position (occupied by *-geard*). Let us assume that the constraints applying to compounds apply also to any word group that mimics the structure of a compound. This assumption, together with rule (3b), explains why verses like (5a) do not occur. Division of (5a) according to natural constituency yields a second foot *blōde fāh* in which *fāh* alliterates with *folm* while *blōde,* the first lexical constituent of the foot, fails to alliterate. The verse is unmetrical because its second foot fails to conform to the alliterative pattern set by compounds like *middangeard.* The third of three stressed words in a verse can alliterate, but only if the first two words form a natural constituent. In (5b), *fīf* and *nihta* form a natural constituent, with alliteration on *fīf,* as required. Here *fyrst* is the sole occupant of the second foot, and may alliterate.

Although (3a-b) are consistent with Sievers's treatment of the heavier verse types, our bracketing rules will not allow us to divide certain other verse types as Sievers did:

(6) (a) on an- / cre fæst 303a
         at anchor fast
         "securely anchored"

   (b) Swā rīx- / ode 144a
        thus he-ruled
        "thus he prevailed"

According to Sievers's analysis, (6a) has the verse pattern xS/xS (in our notation) and (6b) has the pattern xS/Sx. These analyses are unacceptable in a word-based theory for two reasons: first, because they involve a foot pattern xS that does not correspond to a word-like phonological unit; and second, because they place the foot boundary inside *ancre* and *rīxode,* where no word boundary occurs.[16] Sievers's division of verses like those in (6) has proved perhaps the most controversial aspect of his theory. It seems particularly inconsistent to require division at the major constituent break in (4) or (5b) while splitting simplex words in (6a-b). Like Pope (1942) and Creed (1966), I assume that the first foot in (6a-b) consists of an unstressed word and that the second foot corresponds to the pattern of an Old English compound. Within our theoretical framework, (6a) has the pattern x/Sxs, and the phrase *ancre fæst* mimics compounds like *middangeard*. Rule (3a) forces division of *Swā rīxode* at the only available word boundary. Verse (6b) is the simplest expression of its underlying pattern x/Sxx, with each foot occupied by a corresponding word.

From our point of view, Sievers's way of dividing the verses makes just the wrong predictions about relative frequency. Consider the following variants of type B:

(7) (a)   geseted ond gesæd 1696a
       set-down and stated
       "set down and stated"

    (b)   Swā giōmor-mōd 2267a
       thus sad-hearted
       "Thus sad-hearted"

If type B verses had two iambic feet, we would expect to find a considerable number of verses consisting of two iambic words, with no extrametrical syllables. Not a single such verse appears in *Beowulf*. There are only two verses in the poem like (7a), which has a pair of iambic words and extrametrical material (the second instance is 1684a). On the other hand, there are over seventy verses like (7b) with a compound of the form Sxs. If we want two-word prototypes for the type B pattern, verses like *Swā giōmor-mōd* are the only plausible candidates.

The distribution of type C variants also tends to support our analysis against that proposed by Sievers:

(8) (a)   belēan mihte 511b
       dissuade might
       "could dissuade"

    (b)   be ȳð-lāfe 566a
       by wave-leavings
       "by the sandy shore"

If type C has the analysis xS/Sx, we would expect the poet to favor verses like (8a), with an "iambic word" followed by a trochaic word. Yet (8a) represents the least common variant of its type. Verses like (8b), with an Ssx compound, occur more than five times as frequently. Verse (8b) is obviously the more plausible two-word prototype for the pattern of (8a-b).[17]

1.6 Extrametrical Words

Our theoretical framework forces us to take a view of extrametrical syllables somewhat different from that adopted by Sievers. Consider the following, for example:

(9) (a) (ge-)wāc æt wīge 2629a
        failed in combat
        "failed in combat"

  (b) þegnas (syndon ge-) þwǣre 1230a
        thanes are united
        "the retainers are united"

  (c) wēox un(der) wolcnum 8a
        waxed beneath clouds
        "flourished under heaven"

In Sievers's terminology, the parenthesized prefix of (9a) is said to stand in *anacrusis*. Syllables in anacrusis do not occupy positions in metrical patterns. In (9b), on the other hand, Sievers would regard the parenthesized elements as occupants of the first *thesis* in the metrical pattern, which can contain one or more unstressed syllables. Sievers makes no distinction between the status of *syndon ge-* in (9b) and the status of *-der* in (9c): in both cases, the parenthesized elements are regarded as optional material included within the metrical pattern. The theory proposed here, which regulates the number of unstressed syllables lying within the foot, requires a different approach. Because no native Old English words have a stressed syllable followed by four unstressed syllables, no models exist for a foot of the form Sxxxx. We must regard the parenthesized elements in (9b) as lying outside the foot, like syllables in anacrusis. According to rule (3a), moreover, every foot boundary must coincide with a word boundary. Committed to this rule, we cannot include the first syllable of *under* within the foot while excluding its second syllable. Sievers would analyze (9c) as a variant of the Sx/Sx pattern with an optional syllable in the thesis; but for us (9c) represents a distinct pattern Sxx/Sx.

Putting aside certain details for later discussion, we can formulate the rule for extrametrical syllables as below:

(10) Extrametrical words may appear before either foot,[18] subject to certain restrictions on overall verse complexity.

As a kind of encrustation that obscures the underlying design, the extrametrical word will add to complexity. The poet will be careful to avoid or minimize the use of extrametrical words when he employs certain verse patterns that are complex in other ways. Note that only unstressed *words* can be extrametrical. If part of a word counts as a member of a foot, all of its unstressed syllables must occupy metrical positions. This departure from Sievers's theory is not just a matter of notation. We shall see in Chapter 3 that rule (10) tolerates a number of verses emended by Sievers. It is interesting to note that the treatment of extrametrical syllables as literally outside the meter, rather than as constituents of basic patterns, seems to be necessary for later English verse forms as well (see Kiparsky 1977, 234).

1.7 A List of Allowable Foot Pairings

We are now in a position to list the reliably attested verse patterns found in *Beowulf,* as represented within the theory proposed here. For convenience, I supply the familiar Sievers type for each pattern,[19] though of course I reject Sievers's assignment of subtypes to five "basic" types. Each of the twenty-five verses below represents a distinct pairing of foot patterns, and as such corresponds to a unique type. I have arranged the types according to length (number of metrical positions) and weight (number of S or s positions), beginning with those in which the first foot is relatively light and short.

Pattern	Sievers Type	Example
x/Sxx	C	Swā / bealdode 2177a thus he-showed-bravery "Thus he showed bravery"
x/Ssx	C	be / ȳð-lāfe 566a by wave-leavings "by the seashore"

The Foot

Pattern	Sievers Type	Example
x/Sxs	B	Swā / giōmor-mōd 2267a thus sad-heart "Thus sad in heart"
x/Sxxs	B	on / fēonda geweald 808a into demons' power "into the power of demons"
xx/Sx	A3	(Ic) hine / cūðe 372a I him knew "I knew him"
xx/Ss	A3	(Mē) þone / wæl-ræs 2101a me that slaughter-rush "To me (for) that attack"
xx/Sxx	C	Þenden / rēafode 2985a meanwhile plundered "meanwhile (each) plundered"
xx/Ssx	C	ofer / hron-rāde 10a over whale-road "over the sea"
xx/Sxs	B	hwæðer / collen-ferð 2785a whether bold-spirit (acc.) "whether . . . the bold one"
xx/Sxxs	B	ofer / geofenes begang 362a over ocean's expanse "over the expanse of ocean"
S/Sxx	Da	lāst / scēawedon 132b track they-examined "they examined the track"
S/Ssx	Da	fēond / man-cynnes 164b enemy of-mankind "enemy of mankind"
S/Sxs	Db	flet / innan-weard 1976b hall-floor inwards "the floor inside the hall"

Pattern	Sievers Type	Example
S/Sxxs	Db	swefan / sibbe-gedriht 729a to-sleep band-of-kinsmen "a band of kinsmen sleeping"
Sx/Sx	A1	furþur / fēran 254a further to-proceed "to proceed further"
Sx/Ss	A2	wīges / weorð-mynd 65a war's worth-memory "glory in warfare"
Sx/Sxx	Dax	Bēowulf / maðelode 405a Beowulf spoke "Beowulf spoke"
Sx/Ssx	Dax	sīde / sǣ-næssas 223a ample sea-nesses "large headlands"
Sx/Sxs	Dbx	enta / ǣr-geweorc 1679a giants' former-work "ancient work of the giants"
Sx/Sxxs[20]	Dbx	oncȳð / eorla gehwǣm 1420a grief of-earls to-each "a grief to every nobleman"
Ss/Sx	A2	fela-hrōr / fēran 27a much-vigorous to-go "going in his prime"
Ss/Ss	A2	gūð-rinc / gold-wlanc 1881a battle-man gold-proud "a warrior decked with gold"
Sxx/Sx	A1	þrēatedon / þearle 560a they-harassed severely "they severely harassed"
Sxx/Ss	A2	tryddode / tīr-fæst 922a stepped glory-fast "the glorious one advanced"

Pattern	Sievers Type	Example
Ssx/S	E	sinc-fāge / sel 167a
		treasure-shining hall
		"hall shining with treasure"

1.8 Nonexistent Feet and Unmetrical Verses

Certain patterns rejected arbitrarily by Sievers are ruled out by principle I:

(11) (a) *gegaf gūð-rinc
wanton warrior
"depraved warrior"
[xS/Ss]

(b) *sē wæs betera ðonne hēo (cf. 469b)
he was better than she
"he was more noble than she"
[xx/Sxxxs]

Because Sievers employs feet of the form xS, corresponding to forms with prefixes like *gegaf,* he has no principled basis for excluding an xS/Ss verse pattern corresponding to (11a). Within our theory, the absence of verses like (11a) follows from the definition of unstressed prefixes as function words. If there is no xS foot pattern, there can be no xS/Ss verse pattern (cf. section 1.4). We do allow unstressed constituents like *ge-* to constitute "light feet" with an x pattern, since they have a status similar to that of words like *ond;* but division after *ge-* in (11a) would yield a second foot of the form Sss, which does not correspond to an Old English compound pattern.[21] Our theory interprets (11a) as x/S/Ss or, if the first syllable is regarded as extrametrical, as (x)S/Ss. The former pattern has three feet, and violates principle II. The latter pattern falls below the minimum size of four metrical positions, perhaps the most widely acknowledged constraint in the metrical system.

Sievers (1885, 241–2) notes that in his type B the number of unstressed syllables occupying the second thesis (between the stresses) never exceeds two. Apparent exceptions are explained by a rule of elision that treats two adjacent unstressed vowels as one.

Example (11b), in which no elision can take place, represents an unattested pattern. The five-types theory, which lacks formal procedures for enumerating the syllables of the thesis, provides no natural way to express this restriction; but within the framework proposed here, it falls out as a straightforward consequence of the most general principles. Because we have no feet of the form xxS or xxxS, Sievers's analysis (xxS/xxxS) is ruled out. For us, the most straightforward analysis of (11b) is xx/Sxxxs, with clause-final *hēo* standing in for the secondary constituent of a compound. As we observed in section 1.4, however, there are no Old English compounds with the pattern Sxxxs. Hence the pattern xx/Sxxxs is unmetrical. It would not help matters to exclude the first two unstressed words as extrametrical syllables. A verse pattern (xx)Sxxx/S is unacceptable because the first foot does not correspond to an Old English word pattern. Exclusion of ðonne as extrametrical would yield the pattern (xx)Sx(xx)S, which has only three metrical positions. If ðonne were replaced by two function words, we could exclude one of them to obtain the pattern (xx)Sxx/(x)S. However, as we shall see in the next chapter, this pattern is equally unacceptable.

2

THE VERSE

2.1 Identification of Verse Patterns

In iambic pentameter, the poet provides variety by deviation from a single underlying verse pattern that iterates a single foot pattern (cf. Kiparsky 1977, 189, 194). In Old English poetry, variety in verse patterns results from the variety of foot patterns and from the variety of their possible pairings. Principle II states that verse patterns can be simple or complex, depending on what kind of feet they contain. An underlying foot pattern corresponding to a familiar word pattern will be relatively easy to identify even when the foot contains a word group rather than a single word. A foot pattern corresponding to an unusual word pattern will be relatively difficult to identify. Identifying the underlying pattern is especially problematic in Old English poetry because the poet mixes verse types rather freely instead of repeating them in "runs" or restricting them to certain locations (cf. R. Lehmann 1975).[1] The audience of a Shakespeare play needs to spend only a few moments in determining the meter (assuming that the poet's name does not give it away). After that, the only analytical effort required is the effort of evaluating mismatches to a pattern known in advance. In *Beowulf,* the meter changes unpredictably from verse to verse, and the underlying pattern must be recovered in each case from linguistic material. The matching rules (2–3), which are much stricter than those of iambic pentameter, help to reduce analytical effort in one way by requiring that word groups occupying the foot must conform closely to underlying patterns. In this chapter, we will examine additional constraints that restrict the frequency of complex foot patterns, their pairing with other foot patterns, and their positioning in the verse.

2.2 Some Impossible Verse Patterns

Our theory posits nine distinct foot patterns (see section 1.4). The number of pairings theoretically possible is 9 x 9, or 81, but of these we can immediately exclude from consideration 18 pairings with a second foot of the form x or xx. A foot of the form x or xx would require a clitic occupant, but Old English verses, which have syntactic integrity, do not end in proclitics (see Introduction, note 1). Function words employed at the end of the verse almost always acquire a stress that prevents their root syllables from occupying x positions.[2] Since restrictions on the syntax of verses eliminate x and xx from second position independently, we need not duplicate that result with restrictions on foot pairing.

2.3 Overlap

We can also eliminate the pairing Sxx/S from consideration. Its absence is due to a general constraint on foot patterns:

(12)   Foot patterns may not overlap verse patterns.

Refer once again to the list of foot patterns in section 1.4. Note that although the list includes feet corresponding to words like *middangeard*, it does not include feet corresponding to inflected forms of these large compounds (e.g. *middangeardes*, with the pattern Sxsx). In *Beowulf*, words like *middangeardes* appear as complete normal verses rather than as feet. Rule (3) allows for this possibility by stipulating that compounds may count as two words. Moreover, rule (2c) will allow a syllable of secondary stress to occupy an S position in the second foot.[3] Hence *middangeardes* qualifies as an Sx/Sx verse (Sievers type A1). Consider what would happen if the meter did allow feet of the form Sxsx to occur freely.[4] In that case, words like *middangeardes* could occupy either the foot pattern Sxsx or the verse pattern Sx/Sx. Word groups like *gomban gyldan,* which constitute Sx/Sx verses (cf. (1a)), could also constitute Sxsx feet. The result would be extreme confusion about the number of feet. Such confusion would be perceived by the audience as a faltering of the meter because the number of feet is the only constant factor at the level of the verse (cf. principle II). Similarly, if verse patterns of the form Sxx/S were allowed, a word like *sibbegedriht* could represent an Sxxs foot or an Sxx/S verse. To maintain the sense of a two-word norm, the poet standardizes interpretation of compounds with respect to feet. Compounds similar in size to simplex words are interpreted as one foot. Those that match useful two-word verse patterns are interpreted as two feet.

The employment of compounds like *sibbegedriht* as one foot, despite their length, may not be entirely arbitrary. Consider the simpler expressions of a verse pattern Sxx/S, in which each foot would correspond to a single word. One example might be *Bīowulfes biorh,* "Beowulf's barrow," which actually does occur as line 2807a, but not as an Sxx/S pattern. The "reduced stress" on the medial syllable of *Bīowulfes* is eligible for occupation of an s position, and the verse may therefore be scanned as Ssx/S, Sievers type E. Within the framework proposed here, it is difficult to imagine a verse pattern whose simplest two-word expressions qualify as instances of another pattern. Implementation of an Sxx/S pattern would require a restriction preventing verses like 2807a from occupying the Ssx/S pattern; and I can think of no natural way to formulate such a restriction. The poet indicates unmetricality of the Sxx/S verse type by avoiding unambiguous expressions of that type such as *sweorda gelāc* "play of swords," where an inflectional ending and an unstressed prefix stand between two stressed root syllables.[5] A linguistic pattern of this kind is employed as a foot when it appears in *Beowulf* (cf. ðonne / *sweorda gelāc* 1040a, an xx/Sxxs pattern). The existence of an Sxxs foot pattern gives the poet considerable freedom with respect to placement of phrases like *Bīowulfes biorh.* These may occupy the verse pattern Ssx/S or the foot pattern Sxxs. Strict constraints on anacrusis (discussed in sections 3.3 and 3.4) eliminate any possibility of confusion about the number of feet.

2.4 A Coherent Set of Reliably Attested Patterns

A total of 62 possible pairings remain to be considered. We can represent these conveniently by using a 9 x 7 matrix:

Second Foot

	S	Sx	Ss	Sxx	Ssx	Sxs	Sxxs
x				X	X	X	X
S				X	X	X	X
xx		X	X	X	X	X	X
Sx		X	X	X	X	X	X
Ss		X	X				
Sxx		X	X				
Ssx	X						
Sxs							
Sxxs							

First Foot

2.5 Constraints on Deviation from the Norm

Foot patterns represented on the matrix are arranged according to length and weight. "X" markings indicate verse patterns reliably attested in *Beowulf*. The X's in the top row, for example, correspond to the first four patterns listed in section 1.7: x/Sxx, x/Ssx, x/Sxs, and x/Sxxs. We must now consider why just those pairings indicated by X's, and no others, are acceptable to the poet.

Note the strikingly coherent clumping of X's toward the upper right area of the chart, which suggests systematic deviation from a norm. Within the framework of principles I and II, the simplest foot pattern is Sx, corresponding to the most common word pattern. The simplest verse pattern is therefore Sx/Sx. This pattern, which corresponds to Sievers's type A1, is an obvious candidate for the norm, since it has by far the highest relative frequency (cf. Sievers 1885, 235–6, 275–6). What we need, then, is a way of characterizing deviation from the Sx foot pattern and from the Sx/Sx verse pattern. Let us refer to Sx as the *standard foot*. In relation to this standard, a foot with one metrical position will be *short* and a foot with three or more metrical positions will be *long*. A simple pair of rules will now account for most of the empty spaces at the upper left and lower right of the chart:

(13) (a) A short foot must be paired with a long foot.

    (b) Only one foot may be long.

Rule (13a) expresses the familiar constraint against verses with less than four metrical positions as a constraint on deviation from the Sx/Sx norm.[6] The desire to avoid overlap is probably responsible for the severity of the restriction. A verse with three metrical positions would be comparable in size to several types of uncompounded words, which must generate feet. Rule (13b) declares unmetrical such verse patterns as Sxx/Sxx, Sxx/Sxxs, etc. As we shall see in section 6.3, (13b) establishes a no-man's-land between normal and hypermetrical verses, eliminating the possibility of overlap at the other end of the scale. There is no need for a categorical requirement that a long foot be accompanied by a short foot.

In many familiar meters, the foot corresponds to a stressed simplex word. Old English verse employs two unusual types of feet: *light feet* corresponding to words without stress and *heavy feet* corresponding to compounds with two stressed root syllables. The *Beowulf* poet shows a marked tendency to balance long heavy feet against light feet. We find almost two balanced pairings (verses of the form x/Ssx, x/Sxs, etc.) for every combination of a long heavy foot with an S or Sx foot (e.g. S/Ssx, S/Sxs). Because Old English verses do not end in proclitics, light feet can appear only in first position. This means that heavy feet normally appear in second position.

Within the group of heavy feet our principle of complexity makes further distinctions. Usually the first constituent of an Old English compound will consist of a single long syllable or of two short syllables, and the second constituent will have an overt inflectional ending. The foot pattern Ssx corresponds to the normative compound pattern; the foot pattern Ss to a compound pattern of lower frequency; and the foot patterns Sxs, Sxxs to compound patterns of the lowest frequency.

The simpler heavy feet Ssx and Ss need not occupy the normal position for compounds, but may also appear in the first foot of *reversed* half-lines. The long heavy feet Sxs and Sxxs, which correspond to unusual word patterns, always appear in second position. Apparently these more complex feet would be too difficult to perceive in an unexpected location. Consider the following, for example:

(14) (a) wræc / Wedera nīð 423a
          I-avenged the-Weders' injury
          "I avenged the injury to the Weders"

     (b) *Wedera nīð / wræc
          the-Weders' injury I-avenged
          "I avenged the injury to the Weders"

     (c) Hēo þā / fæhðe wræc 1333b
          she the injury avenged
          "she avenged the injury"

Verse (14a), divided according to the syntax, exemplifies the pattern S/Sxs, with the complex Sxs foot occupying its normal location. The word order of (14b) is quite acceptable, as (14c) shows, but (14b) imposes a severe analytical burden on the audience. The form *Wedera* is obligatorily interpreted as the metrical sequence Sx, with resolution of the short stressed syllable.[7] Because the standard foot is Sx, and the standard verse is Sx/Sx, the audience will tend to perceive *Wedera* as a foot. The natural constituent *Wedera nīð*, with alliteration on the root syllable of *Wedera*, matches the foot pattern Sxs. Since Sxs corresponds to an unusual type of compound, this pattern will be difficult to perceive as a foot when occupied by a word group, especially if alternative analyses suggest themselves. Confronted with (14b), the audience would be strongly tempted to divide the verse after the verse-initial trochaic word; but that impulse would conflict with (3b), which requires division at the major constituent break (after *nīð*). The poet avoids the pattern of (14b) to ensure that linguistic material will provide consistent indications of the boundary between feet.

   Let us now consider the heavier verse patterns with respect to their total length. We observe, first, a strong preference for verses of four metrical positions. Short S feet greatly outnumber Sx feet when the other foot in the verse is long and heavy.[8] The avoidance of standard Sx feet in heavy verses shows that the Sx/Sx pattern is genuinely normative. One cannot explain its high relative frequency solely by reference to the frequency of the trochaic words it accommodates. Note that there are no reversed half-line patterns such as Ssx/Sx, Ssx/Ss, or Ss/Sxx. The extra length, in combination with the unexpected order of feet, renders such patterns unacceptably complex.[9]

We can now express the constraints on heavy verses as constraints on reversed half-line patterns:

(15) (a)   Reversed half-line patterns may not contain a foot of the form Sxs or Sxxs.

    (b)   Reversed half-line patterns may not exceed normative length.

2.6 The Importance of Generalized Constraints

The rules given above capture the most widely acknowledged constraints on Old English half-lines. It should be emphasized, however, that the concept of "verse type" employed by Sievers plays no significant role within the framework of principles I-II. Sievers justifies his theory by showing that the attested verses can be analyzed as instances of a relatively small number of "basic types" (A, B, C, D, and E). Assignment of "subtypes" to "basic types" accordingly plays a major role, and it is just this feature of the theory that has sustained the most severe criticism. Bliss (1958) devotes a great deal of his effort to showing that there are more than five "basic types." Our approach has been to argue that the poet uses as many foot patterns and verse patterns as possible. Every word-unit with phonological significance generates a foot pattern. All twenty-five verse patterns exist as distinct types graded in complexity according to their deviation from a single Sx/Sx norm. Rules that govern the matching of linguistic material to metrical patterns apply generally, without distinguishing one type from another.

Our theory also differs markedly from Sievers's with respect to its isolation of unmetrical verses. Since the five-types theory allows for subtypes of low frequency, the cut-off point between complex verses and unmetrical verses is arbitrary. Any limited corpus will contain statistical anomalies: A phonological pattern attested five times as a verse in *Beowulf* might not be more complex, from a metrical point of view, than one attested twenty times. Within the framework adopted here, which employs generalized constraints in the form of categorical rules, any unmetrical verse differs from *all* metrical verses in one or more fundamental ways. A handful of exceptions to rules applying crucially in thousands of cases can be rejected with some confidence as unmetrical.[10] We shall see in Chapter 10 that the number of exceptions to our theory falls well within the expected range, implying a rather high standard of scribal accuracy.

3

LIGHT FEET AND EXTRAMETRICAL WORDS

3.1 Long Strings of Function Words

The foot patterns of our theory include xx, Sxx, and Sxxs, with two adjacent x positions. No foot or pair of feet will provide three adjacent x positions, however. A meter flexible enough for epic storytelling must of course allow for the long strings of function words that occur in a variety of Old English syntactic constructions. Hence extrametrical words arise.

Although sequences of three or more adjacent unstressed syllables cannot well be avoided, the poet can select certain verse patterns as preferred locations for such sequences. In this chapter, we will consider how the poet deploys unstressed words.

3.2 Anacrusis and Light Feet

Unstressed syllables preceding the first stressed word of the half-line will be interpreted in one of two quite different ways. In some cases, such syllables count as extrametrical; in other cases, they signal the presence of a light x or xx foot. The audience must arrive at the correct interpretation in order to determine the number of feet. An important restriction that reduces analytical effort confines long strings of function words to the lighter verse patterns A3, B, and C. Verse types with an S position in the first foot usually have no anacrusis, sometimes a single syllable in anacrusis, very rarely two syllables.[1] A string of three or more unstressed verse-initial syllables will always signal the presence of an x or xx foot. Confronted with such a string, one can assign the first alliterating syllable of the verse unhesitatingly to its second foot.[2] Actually, the use of anacrusis is more restricted than this general account implies (cf. Cable 1974, 32–44). Even in the normative type A1, anacrusis generally involves unstressed prefixes, which are more difficult to manipulate than other function words. Any non-prefixal function word at the beginning of the verse therefore provides a rather reliable indication of a light foot.

3.3 Constraints on Anacrusis in Complex Verses

Because anacrusis aggravates the complexity of heavy verses, we would expect severe restrictions on anacrusis where complex heavy patterns such as Ssx/S are concerned. In fact, anacrusis does not occur with reversed patterns at all. This categorical restriction is quite easy to motivate in perceptual terms. Recall that the metrical system favors "balanced" combinations of light feet and heavy feet, especially where long heavy feet are concerned.[3] The favored verse pattern x/Ssx corresponds exactly to the forbidden verse-initial sequence (x)Ssx/ . . . , where (x) stands in anacrusis. A verse pattern (x)Ssx/S would have a false sense of closure at the verse-medial boundary, creating confusion about the number of feet. Since the Ssx/S pattern is already very complex, such confusion is intolerable.

The restriction against anacrusis in reversed half-lines excludes verses like the following:

(16)   *(ge)swincdagum / swearc (cf. 1993a)
       in-days-of-suffering darkened
       "became gloomy in days of suffering"

The compound form *geswincdagum* did not have general currency, and therefore did not undergo weakening to "reduced stress" of the root syllable in its secondary constituent.[4] Hence (16) must be interpreted as (x)Ssx/S, an unmetrical pattern.

3.4 Interpretation of Borderline Cases

Because the Old English poet employs so many different verse types, a complex variant of one type often resembles a variant of another type. By avoiding unambiguous violations of constraints on anacrusis, the poet signals the proper interpretation of certain borderline cases that would otherwise cause confusion. Consider the following:

(17) (a)   Bīowulfes / biorh 2807a
        Beowulf's barrow
        "Beowulf's barrow"
        [Ssx/S]

    (b)   wæs him / Bēowulfes sīð 501b
        was to-him Beowulf's adventure
        "Beowulf's adventure was to him"
        [(x)x/Sxxs]

The compound proper noun form spelled *Bēowulfes* or *Bīowulfes,* with "reduced stress" on the medial syllable, corresponds to metrical Sxx and also to metrical Ssx. In (17a), *Bīowulfes* must occupy an Ssx foot because (12) rules out the pattern Sxx/S. In (17b), on the other hand, *Bēowulfes* must occupy the Sxx portion of an (x)x/Sxxs pattern, since there are no normal verses like (16) to serve as paradigms for a pattern (xx)Ssx/S.[5]

Our theory allows for the verse pattern xx/Sx (type A3), and it also tolerates verses of the form (xx)Sx/Sx (type A1 with anacrusis). In the latter type one might expect a false sense of closure at the medial foot boundary, but the poet takes special steps to avoid such confusion:

(18) (a)   (gē æt) hām gē / (on) herge 1248a
        both at home and in the-field
        "both at home and in the field"
        [(xx)Sx/(x)Sx]

    (b)   ðē wē / ealle 941a
        which we all
        "which we all"
        [xx/Sx]

The freedom to employ type A1 verses like (18a) is defended by restricting the number of type A3 verses like (18b), which has the minimum number of syllables. Less than five percent of A3 verses resemble (18b); the rest have one or more extrametrical words. Since the audience sees the syllabic sequence xxSx so seldom as a verse, it will experience no false sense of closure in verses like (18a), with the (xx)Sx/(x)Sx pattern.[6] The use of extrametrical words to indicate the presence of a light foot turns what might seem a necessary evil into a positive good. In type A3, extrametrical words do not obscure the xx/Sx pattern, but help to distinguish it from the initial portion of an (xx)Sx/Sx pattern.

3.5 Constraints on Isolated Prefixes

A verse-initial prefix without accompanying extrametrical words usually counts as anacrusis. Such an isolated prefix may occasionally be employed as a foot in a relatively simple verse pattern, but hardly ever in a verse pattern of significant complexity:

(19) (a) be- / lēan mihte 511b
dissuade might
"could dissuade"
[x/Ssx]

(b) ge- / seted ond gesǣd 1696a
set down and stated
"set down and stated"
[x/Sxxs]

(c) *ofer- / sōhte
overtaxed
"overtaxed"
[xx/Sx]

The *Beowulf* poet employs an isolated prefix as a foot in somewhat more than fifty balanced verses like (19a), where the second foot has the normative compound pattern Ssx. Isolated prefixes appear as feet much less often when the second foot has the complex pattern Sxs or Sxxs: only five verses like (19b) occur in the poem (cf. 34a, 620a, 1870a, 2516a). The absence of verses like (19c) is expected. Such verses would cause even more confusion than those like (18b).

3.6 Anacrusis and Whole-Verse Compounds

We noted in section 2.3 that large compounds like *middangeardes* appear as complete verses. It is interesting to note that such verses never have anacrusis. Balanced half-lines of type B or C often consist of a function word followed by a compound. Apparently an extrametrical word followed by a whole-verse compound would have borne a confusing resemblance to a balanced half-line. Avoiding anacrusis before whole-verse compounds would help the audience to realize that the compound represented two feet rather than one.[7]

3.7 Extrametrical Words in Some Notorious Cruxes

Rule (10) places all extrametrical syllables outside the foot, whether they occur verse-initially or in verse-medial position. This formulation tolerates some verses that cause problems for Sievers:

(20) (a)   gamol-feax / (ond) gūð-rōf 608a[8]
old-haired and war-bold
"grey-haired and brave in battle"
[Ss/(x)Ss, not Ssx/Ss]

(b)   sæcce / (tō) sēceanne 2562a[9]
combat to seek
"to seek combat"
[Sx/(x)Sxx, not Sxx/Sxx]

(c)   Snyredon / (æt-) somne þā 402a
they-hastened together then
"Then they hurried on together"
[Sx/(x)Sxs, not Sxx/Sxs]

If we included the parenthesized syllables within feet, (20a) would violate (15b) and (20b-c) would violate (13b). If we interpret the parenthesized elements as extrametrical, however, the verses have acceptable patterns. One would expect a strong bias against extrametrical words in very long, very heavy verses; but this need not have taken the form of a categorical prohibition.

Sievers must reject verses like (20b-c) in order to capture the restriction against two long feet (13b). He emends the five verses like (20b) in *Beowulf* by replacing inflected infinitives with uninflected infinitives.[10] I would account for *tō* by analogy with the unstressed prefixes employed so often in anacrusis. Like an unstressed prefix, *tō* has a fixed syntactic location in (20b). Only an unstressed prefix could intervene between *tō* and an associated verbal root. Being difficult to manipulate, *tō* appears in unusual positions more often than do movable function words or those subject to optional deletion. Klaeber assigns *þā* of (20c) to the second half-line of *Beowulf* 402, but the result is very odd from a metrical point of view, and creates as many problems as it solves.[11] Within our theory, verses like (20c) are acceptable, though complex.

3.8 Summary

We are now in a position to state the constraints on extrametrical syllables formally:

(21) (a) Unstressed words may appear before either foot, except before the first foot of a reversed half-line or before the first foot of a verse pattern wholly occupied by a compound.

(b) Extrametrical words reduce complexity in verse patterns with a light foot and add to complexity in verse patterns with an S position in the first foot. Note: when the first foot contains an S position, extrametrical syllables in anacrusis cause more complexity than do extrametrical syllables before the second foot.[12]

4

INTERPRETATION OF AMBIGUOUS
LINGUISTIC MATERIAL

4.1 Systematic Exceptions

Some apparent exceptions to constraints on verse patterns involve words with a phonological structure admitting of more than one metrical interpretation. These fall into a few well-defined classes discussed by Sievers (1893, sections 74–87). Here I review Sievers's observations from the vantage point of recent linguistic work.

4.2 Alternative Interpretations of Contract Forms

One type of *prosodic alternation* involves forms like *hēan* in the weak inflectional paradigm of *hēah* "high, noble." The treatment of such forms appears to reflect the organization of the poet's internalized grammar. Let us consider briefly how generative phonology explains predictable alternation in related forms of a given stem. As we noted above in section 1.1.1, the second *h* of *hēah* disappears in *hēan* because of a sound change that deleted *h* between vowels in the earlier form *hēahan*. According to generative phonology, forms like *hēahan* remain accessible to the native speaker even after they die out in speech. A speaker of Old English would have known intuitively, for example, that *hēan* contained an "underlying" stem-final *h*. It would be difficult to overlook the stem-final *h* that survived in a member of the same paradigm, *hēah*. Moreover, the speaker would have encountered other paradigms showing the same alternation between stem-final *h* in forms without overt inflections and loss of *h* in inflected forms (see OEG, sections 234–9). The speaker would have known, in the same sense, that the inflectional ending derived from an underly-

ing *-an*. During this period, no other inflectional ending with final
n occurred, and the ending took the form *-an* rather than *-n* in the
vast majority of cases. Memorizing the large number of contract
forms as isolated exceptions would have required considerable
effort; but contraction operated so consistently that the rule pre-
dicting its occurrence was relatively easy to intuit.[1] Hence generative phonology assumes that the native speaker's grammar contained some underlying forms corresponding to earlier stages of
the language and a set of synchronic rules relating these abstract
representations to the "surface forms" actually uttered. In the case
of *hēan*, the speaker would have learned only one form of the
stem *(hēah-)* and one form of the inflectional ending *(-an)*, together with synchronic rules of h-loss and vowel contraction that
produced *hēan* and a wide variety of other correct surface forms.
Rules posited to explain one type of alternation must of course
interact appropriately with other rules of the synchronic grammar.
On the place of h-loss and vowel contraction within inflectional
phonology, see Kiparsky and O'Neil (1976).

Contract forms like *hēan* still counted as disyllabic in some
verses (see Amos 1980, 40–63, for a recent discussion). Consider
the following, for example:

(22) (a)   hēan / hūses 116a[2]
           high house's
           "of the noble hall"
           [Sx/Sx, not S/Sx]

    (b)   man ge- / þēon 25b[3]
          a-man to-prosper
          "for a man to prosper"
          [Sx/Sx, not Sx/S]

    (c)   on / flet tēon 1036b[4]
          onto the-floor to-draw
          "to bring onto the floor"
          [x/Ssx, not x/Ss]

    (d)   dēaþwīc / sēon 1275b[5]
          death-place to-see
          "to see the place of death"
          [Ss/Sx, not Ss/S]

(e)   feorran / (ond) néan 839b[6]
from-far and from-near
"from far and near"
[Sx/(x)Sx, not Sxx/S]

The circumflex indicates a surface *ēa* or *ēo* derived by h-loss and vowel contraction.[7] If the contract forms occupied a single metrical position in the verses above, (22a-d) would violate (13a), which requires pairing of a short foot with a long foot, and (22e) would violate (12), which rules out overlap between foot patterns and verse patterns. If we assume that the contract forms occupy two metrical positions, on the other hand, (22a-e) correspond to well-attested verse types.

On the basis of (22a-e) alone, one might conclude that Old English poetry dates from the period before h-loss occurred. Consider the following verse, however:

(23)   fæderæþelum / (on-)fōn 911a
paternal-rank to-receive
"to inherit the father's rank"
[Ssx/(x)S, not Ssx/(x)Sx]

By resolution, *fæderæþelum* can occupy the foot pattern Ssx. A monosyllabic interpretation of *-fōn* (contracted from *fōhan*) will therefore yield a type E verse with an extrametrical word before the second foot. This kind of verse is reliably attested elsewhere in *Beowulf* (cf. 256a, 455a, 476a). If *-fōn* had its old trochaic value, the result, otherwise unattested, would be a long reversed half-line (cf. (15b)). It seems clear that the poet composed during the period after h-loss, but retained the right to employ metrical values of an earlier age.

4.3 Formal Statement of Prosodic Rules

Kiparsky (1968, 1972) made a special study of alternations in metrical value analogous to those in (22) and (23), drawing his data from Finnish and Vedic poetry. According to Kiparsky, the archaic forms used as prosodic alternants correspond to underlying forms in a synchronic grammar of the later poet's language.

Because all native speakers have intuitive access to such abstract representations, poet and audience can understand anomalous formulas of archaic verse as systematic exceptions. Kiparsky explains the poet's ability to employ prosodic alternants in terms of *prosodic rules* with the following general form:

> Prosodic rule (optional)
> Disregard rule X.

This allows for use of archaic forms and also of the forms that replaced them. Applying Kiparsky's schema to the problem at hand, we obtain the following rule for Old English:

(24) PR1 (optional)
      Disregard the rule of vowel contraction.[8]

4.4 Alternative Interpretations of Epenthetic Vowels

Old English scribes spelled words containing postconsonantal *l, m, n, r* with or without epenthetic vowels. Thus we find either *māðm* "treasure" or *māððum, wǣpn* "weapon" or *wǣpen*, with some spellings suggesting a monosyllabic interpretation and others suggesting a bisyllabic interpretation. Such words have two possible prosodic readings as well:

(25) (a) māðþụm-fæt / mǣre 2405a[9]
          treasure-vessel famous
          "a famous vessel of great value"
          [Ss/Sx, not Sxs/Sx]

  (b) morgẹn-longne / dæg 2894a[10]
       morning-long day
       "the whole morning long"
       [Ssx/S, not Sxsx/S]

  (c) sinc-māðþụm / sēlra 2193a[11]
       precious-treasure nobler
       "more noble treasure"
       [Ss/Sx, not Ssx/Sx]

(d) wæl-fāgne / wintẹr 1128a
     slaughter-stained winter
     "winter defiled with slaughter"
     [Ssx/S, not Ssx/Sx]

(e) wīg ofer / wǣpen 685a
     war without weapons
     "war without weapons"
     [Sxx/Sx, not Sxx/S]

Klaeber (1950) underdots the epenthetic vowels in (25a-d) to indicate that such vowels do not count in the scansion. If the underdotted vowels occupied weak positions, rules (15a-b) would exclude (25a-d) as unmetrical. In (25e), on the other hand, the epenthetic vowel of *wǣpen* must occupy a weak position. Otherwise, the verse would overlap the foot pattern Sxxs, in violation of (12). Kiparsky and O'Neil (1976, 533–4) represent postconsonantal liquids and nasals like those in (25) as underlying nonsyllabic consonants that become syllabic by a rule of epenthesis. We can therefore account for the variant forms with a second prosodic rule:

(26) PR2 (optional)
      Disregard the rule of epenthesis.

4.5 Dating Paradoxes

The relatively larger number of examples requiring archaic forms in (22) and (25) above may suggest that vowel contraction and epenthesis began to occur just before the composition of the poem. Such appearances may be deceptive. The *Beowulf* poet employed a formulaic diction with a vocabulary and syntax characteristic in many respects of a much earlier period (cf. Klaeber 1950, lxiii, xci-iv). To a considerable extent, therefore, the persistence of archaic forms might reflect the influence of tradition on a poet composing well after the occurrence of the sound changes in question. Underlying representations in a synchronic grammar of a given period sometimes correspond to forms that disappeared from speech hundreds of years previously.[12]

Old English Meter and Linguistic Theory

4.6 The Poet's Feeling for Language

The assumption that the metrical system of *Beowulf* includes rules like PR1 and PR2 tends to raise our estimate of the poet's competence. Traditional views of metrical alternation have implied some confusion on the part of the poet during a period when a sound change was under way or just completed. As W. P. Lehmann observed (1967, 149–50), "such apparent variation in usage would suggest an uncertainty in either metrics or language which we find scarcely credible." Lehmann's way out of the quandary was simply to accept as infrequent types those otherwise unattested patterns that indicate metrical alternation. Kiparsky's approach makes it possible to state stricter constraints on verse types without any implied criticism of the poet's feeling for language.

4.7 Metrical Alternants

Kiparsky (1977, 239) distinguishes sharply between prosodic rules and *metrical rules*. Prosodic rules, cognate with phonological rules of the poet's internalized grammar, assign varying interpretations to linguistic material. Metrical rules, strictly so-called, specify that certain relations must obtain between interpreted linguistic material and metrical patterns. The alternants associated with a metrical rule do not correspond to underlying forms in the poet's grammar. Typically, such *metrical alternants* have a phonological structure that does not conform exactly to any one idealized pattern, but conforms approximately to more than one pattern.

4.8 Formal Rules for Resolution

A resolvable sequence in an Old English word always generates a single metrical position (cf. section 1.3). As idealized word patterns, the metrical feet employed by the *Beowulf* poet contain no positions analogous to short stressed syllables. We must now consider the relation between abstract feet and the linguistic material of actual verses. As before, we define this type of relation in terms of matching rules that permit deviation from the norm at a cost in complexity:

(27) (a) A short syllable bearing primary stress normally undergoes resolution.

    (b) A short syllable on an S position normally undergoes resolution.

    (c) When more than one metrical position in a verse may contain a resolved sequence, resolution is obligatory on the first such position.

Note that (27a) does not apply to root vowels of constituents subordinated in compounds. Because such root vowels underwent some degree of shortening, secondary stress does not always imply length (cf. OEG, section 90). A short syllable with secondary stress is therefore less of an anomaly than a short syllable bearing primary stress. Short syllables with secondary stress may undergo resolution or may stand unresolved at little or no cost in complexity.[13] Rule (27b) resembles (27a), but applies to metrical positions rather than to linguistic material. It is unusual for an S position to be wholly occupied by a short vowel even when that vowel occurs in a subordinated constituent.

In many cases (27a) and (27b) have the same effect. When a foot is occupied by a word group, however, (27a) and (27b) may apply independently of one another. Consider the following:

(28) (a) on / bearm scipes 35b
       in the-bosom of-the ship
       "in the ship's hold"
       [x/Ssx, not x/Ss]

    (b) heard / hēr cumen 376a
       bold here come
       "the bold one having come here"
       [S/Ssx, not S/Ss]

    (c) þēod- / cyninga 2a
       of-the-nation-kings
       "of the high kings"
       [S/Ssx, not S/Ss]

    (d) feorh / cyninges 1210b[14]
       life of-the-king

"the king's life"
[S/Sxx, not S/Sx]

(e) Hrēðel / cyning 2430b[15]
Hrethel king
"King Hrethel"
[Sx/Sx, not Sx/S]

(f) Wæs mīn / fæder 262a[16]
was my father
"my father was"
[xx/Sx, not xx/S]

In (28a-f), resolution of short stressed syllables would leave no
linguistic material available to fill the fourth metrical position
required by (13a). Examples (28a-b) show a short syllable with
primary stress standing unresolved on the s position. These contravene (27a) but not (27b). Example (28c), with a syllable of
secondary stress standing unresolved on the S position, contravenes (27b) but not (27a). Only a very few verses like (28d-f)
occur. These contravene both (27a) and (27b); hence their limited
distribution.

Rule (27c) usually requires the first resolvable sequence in a
verse to occupy a single S position. If resolution applied optionally
in every case, interpretation of most verse patterns would become
quite a complicated matter. Analysis of each resolvable sequence
would have to take into account all the other possibilities of resolution in the half-line. In most cases, therefore, standardizing interpretation of the first resolvable sequence performs the necessary
function of limiting analytical effort. The A3 pattern stands out as
exceptional because it provides only one metrical position on
which resolution can occur. There is less need to standardize interpretation of the first and only resolvable sequence in a verse like
(28f).[17]

5

RELATIVE FREQUENCY AND METRICAL COMPLEXITY

5.1 Obstacles to Statistical Studies

The most conspicuous limitations on verse patterns imposed by our theory are those categorical rules that forbid two or more deviations from the norm within a single verse. We find long patterns and reversed patterns in considerable numbers, but no long reversed patterns. The complex feet Sxs and Sxxs appear quite frequently in their normal location, but never as the first foot. Verse-initial extrametrical syllables, common with light and balanced patterns, do not occur at all with reversed patterns. It can be much more difficult to isolate the factors that govern the relative frequency of attested types or the relative frequency of variants within a single type. In general, deviation from the norm causes complexity; and complex verses occur less frequently than do simpler verses, all other things being equal.[1] Unfortunately, a corpus of verses that differ only with respect to the feature of interest will often be too small to yield reliable statistics.[2] We must also bear in mind the *Beowulf* poet's fondness for metrical variety, as witnessed by a reluctance to repeat a given verse type twice in succession (see R. Lehmann 1975). This stylistic trait implies a systematic exploitation of the moderately complex types, including the heavier type D and E patterns with four metrical positions. In some cases, of course, deviation from the two-word norm is a practical necessity. Extrametrical syllables occur not because the poet seeks metrical variety but because storytelling in verse demands the employment of function-word strings that arise in a number of Old English sentence structures.

Despite such difficulties, the view of metrical complexity advocated here can explain many anomalies in the distribution of Old English half-lines.

5.2 Diverse Sources of Complexity

Let us review briefly the types of complexity discussed thus far. One fundamental type involves deviation from underlying foot patterns. When a group of words occupies the foot, or when a short stressed syllable stands unresolved, recovery of the underlying pattern requires a kind of effort not required when the foot contains a single word with a straightforward metrical interpretation. Feet corresponding to unusual word patterns represent another important cause of complexity. These are relatively difficult to perceive, especially when occupied by word groups. At the level of the half-line we have to reckon with the kind of complexity that results when a verse pattern deviates from the Sx/Sx norm. The types farthest from this norm are intolerant of additional complexity. Finally, we noted special constraints that prevent confusion about the number of feet in the verse. The poet employs extrametrical words, for example, only where they are not likely to be confused with light feet.

All these types of complexity relate directly to fundamental principles of the theory. From a systematic point of view, principles I, II and their associated corollaries present a simple and straightforward picture.[3] In particular cases, however, it may not be clear just how these principles apply. Consider the patterns x/Sxx and x/Ssx. The former deviates from the standard verse pattern in that it has only one syllable of significant stress. The latter comes closer to standard weight, but its second foot corresponds to a compound pattern less "word-like" than the simplex pattern Sxx.[4] We seem to lack a straightforward theoretical prediction about the relative complexity of x/Sxx and x/Ssx. An attempt to determine the exact frequency of x/Sxx verses would encounter difficulties of no mean order. Many of the forms that match the Sxx pattern (words like *Bēowulfes* with reduced stress on the medial syllable) also match the pattern Ssx (cf. (17a-b)). The only unambiguous cases of x/Sxx are those in which the word occupying the second foot could not occupy the first foot of a type

48

E pattern Ssx/S.[5] It seems clear, nevertheless, that the pattern x/Sxx is more complex than the pattern x/Ssx. If we employed the least restrictive criteria for assignment to the x/Sxx type, we would still find that the x/Ssx type has a significantly higher frequency.[6] In this case, it seems, the pattern with more nearly normal weight takes precedence over the pattern with a more cohesive second foot.

We might be tempted to conclude that "balanced" verses are in general less complex than "light verses." Consider, however, the patterns xx/Ss and xx/Sx. The least restrictive criteria for xx/Ss patterns would fail to yield more than one for every ten of the form xx/Sx. In this case, the light pattern with the simplex in the second foot seems less deviant than the balanced pattern with the compound. A direct appeal to principle I can resolve the apparent discrepancy. The xx/Sx type takes precedence over xx/Ss because Ss is a somewhat unusual compound pattern and Sx is the most common of the simplex word patterns. On the other hand, x/Ssx, with the most common compound pattern, takes precedence over x/Sxx, with a second foot corresponding to a somewhat unusual simplex pattern.[7]

The low frequency of both xx/Sx and xx/Ss is attributable in part to the foot pattern xx, which corresponds to words like *oþþe*. Such disyllabic function words occur much less frequently than do monosyllabic function words like *ond*. According to principle II, therefore, the pattern xx will create more complexity than will the pattern x. Moreover, the poet normally uses long strings of function words to signal the presence of a light foot in first position, as opposed to anacrusis (section 3.2). Since a light foot normally balances a long foot in second position, strings of function words will normally be interpreted as signals of an x position rather than as signals of an xx position. It will require a special analytical effort to determine that a string of function words represents xx.

5.3 Metrical Closure

Bliss (1958, 4) observed that the b-verses of *Beowulf* are less complex, as a group, than the a-verses. Let us express this observation as a general principle:

(29) Minimize complexity in the second half-line.

Principle (29) allows for considerable variety among b-verses, but restricts or forbids employment of those types requiring the most analytical effort.[8]

We can use (29) to test hypotheses based on the problematic evidence of overall frequency. Consider, for example, the most complex heavy foot patterns, Sxs and Sxxs. As we observed in section 2.5, these pair more often with an S foot than with a standard Sx foot. The "expanded Db" patterns Sx/Sxs and Sx/Sxxs occur about thirty times as a-verses, but never occur as b-verses at all.[9] Such evidence indicates that the restricted frequency of Sx/Sxs and Sx/Sxxs patterns does indeed result from metrical complexity, and not from some unsuspected factor. Rule (29) also responds to the complexity of the light foot xx. The verse pattern xx/Ss, which occurs somewhat less often in *Beowulf* than does Sx/Sxs, never appears as a b-verse. The less rare pattern xx/Sx is also restricted to the first half-line.[10]

According to rule (21b), verse-initial extrametrical words add to complexity when the verse pattern has an S position in the first foot. If (29) interacts with (21b) in the expected way, we should find little or no anacrusis in b-verses. As it turns out, the only b-verses compatible with free employment of extrametrical syllables are those with light or balanced patterns. In the second half-line there are relatively few type A1 patterns with anacrusis, and anacrusis does not seem to occur at all with the heavier patterns. Thus (29) helps to confirm the formulation of (21b) based on frequencies of extrametrical words in different verse types.

5.4 Varying Types of Complexity in Combination

Some statistical anomalies widely regarded as significant involve the interaction of several factors. Here the chain of logic connecting theory to data becomes rather long, and may test the reader's patience. It seems worthwhile to proceed, however, because these anomalies testify to a remarkably accurate feeling for language. The *Beowulf* poet manages somehow to employ every pattern readily analyzable as two feet while avoiding all patterns that would create real confusion.

The potential for confusion in Old English poetry is due primarily to the simple foot pattern rule, which generates feet of varying size and weight. Some feet resemble extrametrical words, while others approach the size of complete verses. The overlap constraint (12) ensures a clear distinction between foot patterns and verse patterns. However, problems of ambiguity can still arise with respect to interpretation of linguistic material. The poet is particularly careful in manipulation of short stressed syllables and of verse-initial function words.

5.4.1 Resolution and Enumeration of Feet

Rule (27c), which makes resolution obligatory under certain conditions, differs from the corresponding rule in Sievers's theory, though it often has the same effect. According to Sievers (1885, 230, 243), a resolvable sequence must undergo resolution unless it comes immediately after a stressed syllable (or the resolved equivalent of a stressed syllable). In arguing for this view, Sievers pointed out that an unresolved syllable on the second S position of "type A" generally occurs in the Ss/Sx pattern rather than in the Sx/Sx pattern:

(30) (a)   frum-cyn / witan 252a
           source-family to-know
           "to know the lineage"
           [Ss/Sx]

     (b)   Hrēðel / cyning 2430b
           Hrethel king
           "King Hrethel"
           [Sx/Sx]

It is true that verses like (30a) occur with significant frequency, while those like (30b) are quite rare (cf. section 4.8). Yet it seems to me that the more restricted distribution of verses like (30b) has a cause quite different from the cause posited by Sievers. Consider the following:

(31)   þurh / rūmne sefan 278a
       through large heart
       "with a generous heart"
       [x/Sxs]

At first glance, it might seem possible to analyze (31) as an Sx/Sx pattern with anacrusis. However, anacrusis causes complexity (cf. (21b)). Analysis of (31) as (x)Sx/Sx therefore implies that such verses will occur less frequently than verses like (30b). In fact, verses like (30b) are considerably rarer than verses like (31).[11] Sievers (1885, 291) analyzes (31) as an instance of the balanced type B pattern (x/Sxs in our notation). Under that interpretation, the syllable of primary stress is resolved, and the verse contravenes neither (27a) nor (27b). Hence the higher frequency of verses like (31) relative to those like (30b), which contravenes both norms. Now if the usual interpretation of strings like *Hrēðel cyning* involves resolution of the short stressed syllable, as in *rūmne sefan,* verse (30b) will present the appearance of a single foot, or of an unmetrical verse pattern Sx/S. The fact that such verses occur at all testifies to the priority accorded the normative Sx/Sx pattern, which allows for more complex realizations than does any other verse type. Verse (30a) creates no problems of metrical ambiguity despite its violation of (27a) and (27b). The constituent *-cyn* of *frum-cyn* bears secondary stress, and must occupy an s or S position rather than an x position (cf. (2c)). Assignment of the string *frum-cyn witan* to a single foot would require a nonexistent foot pattern Sss, which does not correspond to an Old English compound pattern. Evidently the violation of (27a) and (27b) is tolerated more often in verses like (30a) because such verses have an unambiguous two-foot structure.

5.4.2 *Peculiarities of the Ss Foot Pattern*

The pattern Ss differs in two important respects from the other compound foot patterns. Pairing of the standard Sx foot with a foot of the form Ssx, Sxs, or Sxxs yields a long verse, but the Ss foot combines with Sx to produce verse types of normative length. Ssx, Sxs, and Sxxs combine with the simplest light foot, x; but the only light foot that can combine with Ss is xx, which requires special analytical effort (cf. section 5.2). In view of the great difference between the complexity of xx and that of Sx, it is not surprising that the poet prefers the heavy Sx/Ss pattern and even the reversed pattern Ss/Sx to the balanced pattern xx/Ss.[12]

The complexity associated with xx, as opposed to Sx, shows up clearly when we examine the poet's employment of an archaic word order:

(32) (a)   *þone / grund-wong
           the ground-plain
           "the bottom"
           [xx/Sx]

     (b)   grund-wong / þone 2588a
           ground-plain the
           "the bottom"
           [Ss/Sx]

     (c)   ǣr hē þone / grund-wong 1496a
           before he the ground-plain
           "before he . . . the bottom" (verb supplied later)
           [(xx)xx/Ss]

     (d)   māgas / þāra 1015b
           kinsmen their
           "their kinsmen"
           [Sx/Sx]

     (e)   *dryhten / þone
           lord the
           "the lord"
           [Sx/Sx]

Note that the variety represented by (32a), with an isolated determiner and no extrametrical syllables, never appears in *Beowulf*.
The determiner þone does appear with a bisyllabic compound in
six verses, but all six have the archaic noun-determiner word
order of (32b).[13] Removed from proclitic position, the determiner
acquires stress, and occupies an Sx foot rather than an xx foot.
The result is a verse of the type represented by (30a), with a short
syllable standing unresolved on the second S position. Archaic
word order would not improve (32c) because ǣr and hē would
remain at the beginning of the verse to violate the constraint
against anacrusis in reversed patterns (21a). An opportunity to
invert the lighter type A3 pattern xx/Sx arises when the determiner
has a long root syllable. In (32d) the etymologically long vowel of
þāra acquires stress when removed from proclitic position. The
result is the simplest variety of type A1. When the bisyllabic determiner has a short radical vowel, inversion of the lighter type A3

pattern would produce the rare type A1 variant represented by (30b). Hence there is no motivation for verses like (32e).

We have frequently observed that the poet avoids complex variants of complex patterns. With less than thirty attestations, the xx/Ss pattern must certainly be regarded as complex, and some imaginable varieties do not occur at all:

(33) (a)   hond ond / heard sweord 2509a
           hand and strong sword
           "a hand and a strong sword"
           [Sx/Ss]

     (b)   *oþþe þæt / heard sweord
           or the strong sword
           "or the strong sword"
           [xx/(x)Ss]

In Sx/Ss verses, the poet can employ a word group like *heard sweord* rather than matching the ideal foot pattern with a bisyllabic compound. In the more complex xx/Ss verses, the second foot always conforms to the ideal pattern. There are no verses like (33b), with a word group in place of a compound.[14]

5.4.3 *Some Problems Involving Resolution and Metrical Closure*

Sievers (1885, 462–3) noticed some interesting anomalies in the placement of short stressed syllables:

(34) (a)   (Hē) on / weg losade 2096b
           He away escaped
           "He got away"
           [(x)x/Ssx]

     (b)   fyll / cyninges 2912b
           fall of-the-king
           "the king's fall"
           [S/Sxx]

     (c)   seomade / (ond) syrede 161a
           lay and ambushed

"lay in wait and ambushed"
[Sx/(x)Sx]

(d) þæt wæs /gōd cyning 11b
that was good king
"that was a good king"
[(x)x/Ssx]

(e) (ne ge-)frægn / (ic) frēond-līcor 1027a
not heard I more amiably
"I never heard . . . more amiably"
[(xx)S/(x)Ssx]
(rest of clause delayed)

Verses like (34a-b) are rare, while those like (34c-d) are quite common. Within the framework employed here, we can say that the poet assigns trisyllabic words like *losade, cyninges, seomade,* and *syrede* preferentially to feet of the form Sx (as in (34c)), rather than assigning them to the sequence sx (as in (34a)) or allowing the short stressed syllable to stand unresolved in an Sxx pattern (as in (34b)). Such a preference is quite understandable for several reasons. In the first place, the standard Sx foot has the least restricted distribution, and provides the greatest number of opportunities for employment of compatible words. Secondly, words like *losade* correspond most closely to the Sx pattern, the pattern that they generate (see section 1.3). A third reason has to do with possible confusion about the metrical significance of unstressed words. Since *weg losade* and *fyll cyninges* have the same range of metrical interpretations, one must determine whether the string *Hē on* occupies extrametrical positions before an S/Sxx pattern or provides a light foot for an (x)x/Ssx pattern. Without a clear signal to indicate the status of *Hē on*, the audience might reject (34a) as an aberrant three-foot pattern (x)x/S/Sxx. It requires a special effort to arrive at the least complex interpretation (x)x/Ssx. The potential for confusion would be even greater if verses like (34e) occurred in considerable numbers. As we noted in section 3.2, however, type Da verses most often have only one syllable in anacrusis, and that syllable is usually an unstressed prefix.

Bisyllabic forms like *cyning* present quite a different picture. These correspond most closely to the foot pattern S, but the S pattern is employed much less frequently than is the standard pattern Sx. On the other hand, there will be frequent opportunities for employment of words like *cyning* to fill an sx sequence because the most common type of compound generates the pattern Ssx. Note that (34d) cannot be confused with verses like (34e). The string *gōd cyning* fills three metrical positions at most, and could not constitute a verse. Hence the relatively high frequency of verses like (34d), as opposed to those like (34a). Sievers's view of resolution does not account at all well for the rarity of verses like (34b). If resolution is optional after a stressed syllable, verses like (34b) should be no more deviant with respect to resolution than those like (34d). The theory proposed here accounts for the discrepancy in terms of (27a) and (27b). Verse (34d) contravenes neither one of these norms, while (34b) contravenes both. It is worth reiterating here that an unresolved syllable occupying the second S position of an S/Sxx pattern usually lies within the subordinated constituent of a whole-verse compound like *þēodcyninga* (cf. (28c)). Such verses contravene (27b) but not (27a).

Principle (29) often restricts complex variants to the first half-line, but the handful of verses like (34a) all appear in the second half-line (see Sievers 1885, 462–3). This paradox resolves itself when we consider that the complexity of (34a) results from potential confusion with verses like (34e), which are excluded from the second half-line by (21b) and (29). As an a-verse competing for attention with (34e), (34a) would be extremely complex; but as a b-verse it is considerably less so. The avoidance of anacrusis in the second half-line makes it easy to identify the light feet of b-verses with balanced patterns.

5.5 Less Significant Forms of Metrical Ambiguity

The poet restricts employment of unstressed words only when they create confusion about the number of feet. In certain cases, such confusion cannot arise:

(35) (a) (Him) þā / hilde-dēor 312a
to-them then the-battle-bold
"To them then the bold one"
[(x)x/Sxs, not xx/Sxs]

(b) wǣron / ȳð-gebland 1620b
    were wave-tossings
    "the tossings of the waves were"
    [xx/Sxs]

(c) secgan / (tō) sōðe 51a
    to-say for truth
    "to say truly"
    [Sx/(x)Sx, not Sxx/Sx]

(d) þrēatedon / þearle 560a
    harassed sorely
    "sorely harassed"
    [Sxx/Sx]

One might interpret (35a) and (35c) as four-position verses with extrametrical words or as five-position verses analogous to (35b) and (35d). For the sake of consistency in presentation, I select the analysis corresponding to the simplest underlying pattern. In (35a), the complexity of the xx foot suggests interpretation as (x)x/Sxs rather than as xx/Sxs. The constraint against splitting simplexes (3a) does require us to posit an xx foot in verses like (35b); but in such verses the light foot will cause no special difficulties of perception, since it will correspond to exactly one word with no extrametrical syllables. Analysis of the xx foot is problematic only in the xx/Sx pattern, where the first foot *must* be analyzed as xx but is typically enmeshed in a long string of function words.[15] I posit an extrametrical syllable in (35c) because the pattern Sx/Sx is simpler than the pattern Sxx/Sx.

Such decisions will affect the relative frequencies obtained in statistical analysis of verse patterns, but may have little or no theoretical significance. Principles I and II place emphasis on recovery of an underlying two-word structure rather than on recovery of any particular metrical pattern. Constraints operating at the level of the half-line serve primarily to prevent confusion about the number of feet, preventing overlap and favoring the foot patterns most easily recognized. If a verse analyzed unambiguously as two feet and if it obviously corresponded to an acceptable pattern, the fact that it qualified as metrical under two interpretations would cause no confusion.

5.6 The Poet's Sensitivity to the Two-Word Norm

The reader who has worked through the examples in this chapter will be impressed, I think, by the poet's skill, which goes far beyond avoidance of metrical lapses. Maximal proliferation of verse patterns might seem incompatible with a clear two-foot structure, but the poet reconciles these stylistic desiderata with remarkable success. Much remains to be said, of course, about the distribution of unstressed words and of metrical alternants. A full account of the poet's stylistic preferences, with appropriate statistical argumentation, would require another volume the size of this one.

6

HYPERMETRICAL VERSES

6.1 Clustering

If certain long half-lines occurred at random in Old English poetry, we would have to regard them as exceptions to rules for
normal types. In fact, the so-called *hypermetrical verses* appear in
clusters that set them apart as distinct types subject to special
constraints. The small number of clusters in *Beowulf* makes detailed analysis somewhat problematic.[1] Evidence from other Old
English poems suggests, however, that the hypermetrical verses of
Beowulf represent the most widespread patterns (for detailed discussion see Pope 1942, 99–115).

6.2 Hypermetrical Patterns in the First Half-line

Most hypermetrical a-verses have a structure like that of the following example from *Beowulf:*

(36) gān under / gyldnum bēage 1163a
      to-walk under golden ring
      "walking adorned with a golden necklace"

Sievers (1893, section 94) analyzes such patterns as normal verses
preceded by an additional foot that usually takes the form Sx or
Sxx. In (36), *gyldnum bēage* corresponds to a normal type A1
verse and *gān under* constitutes an Sxx foot.

The major constituent break of a hypermetrical a-verse comes
between the first and second foot (cf. Bliss 1972, 244). The embedded normal verse generally has a simple structure: standard

patterns like that of *gyldnum bēage* outnumber all others by far. Embedded normal verses also tend to be more cohesive than free-standing normal verses. Outside of hypermetrical clusters, large compounds occupy a whole normal verse quite infrequently, but the ten hypermetrical a-verses of *Beowulf* include the following two:

(37) (a) sǣton / suhtergefæderan 1164a
        sat uncle-nephew-pair
        "the uncle and his nephew sat"

   (b) mon on / middangearde 2996a
        a-man on middle-earth
        "any man on earth"

Metrists who comment on patterns like those in (36) and (37) usually assume that they consist of three feet (cf. Pope 1942, 105). However, the disproportionate number of verses like (37a-b) suggests that the embedded normal verse constitutes a single large foot of the form Sxsx.[2] Under ordinary conditions, the metrical system interprets compounds like those in (37) as Sx/Sx to prevent overlap, but we need not assume the same interpretation for hypermetrical clusters. With respect to theoretical simplicity, moreover, the two-foot analysis seems superior by far. If hypermetrical verses had three feet, they would violate rule II, which defines a verse as a pair of feet.

Let us stipulate that hypermetrical verses obey all the rules for normal verses, with one exception:

(38)   The second foot of a hypermetrical verse overlaps a normal verse pattern with an S position in the first foot.

We now analyze (37a-b) as instances of a pattern Sx/Sxsx in which the second foot overlaps the type A1 pattern Sx/Sx. Example (36) corresponds to a pattern Sxx/Sxsx, with a word group in the second foot. The proximity of other unusually long verses will signal that compounds like *middangearde* and word groups like *gyldnum bēage* count as single *overlapping feet* rather than as two feet.

Hypermetrical Verses

6.3 Hypermetrical Verses and Normal Verses

The location of the major constituent break in hypermetrical a-verses follows from the bracketing rule (3b), which stipulates that assignment of stressed words to feet in heavy verses must respect syntactic constituency (cf. (4–5)). The position of the overlapping foot within the verse is also very much in accord with the poet's usual practice. Overlapping feet correspond to compounds of low frequency, and must be regarded as extremely complex. It seems natural that these feet should appear only in second position, like the complex feet Sxs and Sxxs (cf. (15a)). Overlapping feet vary in complexity according to the frequency of the corresponding large compound (cf. principle I). Since the most common large compound pattern is Sxsx, the Sxsx foot is the simplest member of its complex group. Hence the predominance of Sxsx feet in hypermetrical verses.

The distinct boundary between normal and hypermetrical patterns results in part from (13b), which rules out normal patterns with two long feet:

(39) *sige-hrēþig tryddode
      victory-proud advanced
      "advanced victoriously"

Borderline cases like (39) do not appear among normal verses or in hypermetrical clusters. Hypermetrical verses may have two long feet, but only if the second foot overlaps a normal pattern as specified in (38). An attempt to analyze (39) as a hypermetrical pattern S/Sxsxx would fail because the major constituent break would not coincide with the foot boundary. Rule (3b) allows only the analysis Ssx/Sxx, which violates both (13b) and (38). In general, the restrictions on heavy normal verses ensure that the transition into a hypermetrical cluster will correspond to a perceptible change in average verse size.

6.4 Hypermetrical Patterns in the Second Half-line

Heavy patterns like those in (36) and (37) are excluded from the second half-line by rules for alliteration (discussed below in section 8.7). The typical b-verse encountered in hypermetrical clusters has a structure like that of the following example:

(40) þǣr þā / gōdan twēgen 1163b
      where the good two
      "where the two noble ones"

One might think of analyzing (40) as a type A verse with two syllables in anacrusis. However, this variant is rare even in the first half-line, and never appears in the second half-line outside of hypermetrical clusters. Apparently the interaction of (21b) and (29) rules out a second syllable of anacrusis in the b-verse. Within hypermetrical clusters, therefore, we can assume that two or more unstressed syllables at the beginning of a b-verse signal the presence of a light foot.[3] On this hypothesis, (40) analyzes as xx/Sxsx, and the word group *gōdan twēgen* counts as an overlapping foot.

6.5 Isolated Normal Verses

I assume here that the complexity of hypermetrical patterns makes clustering obligatory for them. Anything resembling an isolated hypermetrical pattern constitutes an exception to the rules for normal verses. Isolated normal verses, however, may occur within hypermetrical clusters:

(41) þæt hē hæfde / mōd micel 1167a
      that he had courage great
      "that he had great courage"

Verse (41) lies within a cluster (or one might say between two clusters). It does not conform to (38), but does correspond to the common type C pattern (xx)xx/Ssx. Evidently the audience could identify relatively simple patterns of this type even in the midst of verses following a somewhat different rule system.

6.6 The Motivation for Hypermetrical Patterns

Sievers's account of hypermetrical verses fails to explain why they should occur. Within the framework proposed here, there is an obvious motivation for the longer patterns. Our first fundamental principle states that feet correspond to words. Since the language does contain large compound words, this principle implies the existence of corresponding large feet. The strategy of clustering makes it possible to employ such feet while preserving a clear two-foot structure. Outside of hypermetrical clusters, the overlap constraint (12) applies in the usual way, rejecting feet that correspond to normal verse patterns.

It is interesting to note that prepositional phrases like *on middangearde* can appear only in hypermetrical verses (cf. (37b)). The preposition *on* could not appear as anacrusis in an (x)Sx/Sx pattern without violation of (21a), which forbids anacrusis before whole-verse compounds. Placing the preposition at the end of the previous verse would be equally impossible because of the constraint against verse-final proclitics (Introduction, note 1). To a certain extent, then, hypermetrical verses may reflect the necessities of storytelling. Certain syntactic structures that the poet wishes to use cannot be accommodated easily as normal verses.

7

ALLITERATION

7.1 The Equivalence Rule

Within the Old English poetic line, a phonological equivalence called *alliteration* gives special prominence to certain stressed syllables. Surviving Old English texts make it clear what kind of similarity counts as alliteration. In most cases, two stressed root syllables with the same initial consonant may be said to alliterate. Thus *beorn* "man" alliterates with *bryd* "wife." Note that the prevocalic *r* in *bryd* is not subject to the identity requirement. Initial *sp-, st-,* and *sc-* alliterate as clusters, however. A word like *stān* "stone," with initial *st-,* alliterates only with words like *strǣt* "street," not with words like *sǣ* "sea" or *spere* "spear." The identity requirement applies exclusively to consonants, never to vowels.[1] Syllables without prevocalic consonants act as if they had a "zero consonant" in initial position (cf. Jakobson 1963). Thus *eorl* "earl" *(Øeorl)* alliterates with *æþelu* "nobility" *(Øæþelu)*.

Kuryłowicz (1970, 13–16) noticed that the syllabic constituents governed by the equivalence rule correspond to those governed by a rule of Germanic grammar. In Gothic, which best preserves the rule of reduplication, the reduplicating syllable is formed by adding a vowel spelled *aí* to the "initial constituent" of the root syllable. When two or more consonants precede the root vowel, as in *slēpan* "to sleep," only the first normally reduplicates (cf. the preterite form *saí-slēp*). As in alliteration, however, the consonant clusters *sp-, st-,* and *sk-* (the latter corresponding to OE *sc-*) count as unitary constituents.[2] Hence *skaidan* "divide" has a preterite *skaí-skaiþ*. The "zero consonant" recognized by the equivalence rule also counts as an initial constituent for purposes of reduplication. Hence *aukan* "increase" *(Øaukan)* has *aí-auk (Øaí-Øauk)* as its preterite.[3]

7.2 Alliteration and the Relative Prominence of Words

Sievers (1893, sections 22–9) noticed that the probability of alliteration for a given syllable depends on the type of word in which that syllable appears. He found three natural word classes differing considerably in their metrical behavior:

(42) Class A: nouns, adjectives, infinitives, and participles.

　　 Class B: adverbs and finite forms of "full verbs" (excluding auxiliaries and the copula).

　　 Class C: function words such as prepositions, conjunctions, pronouns, finite forms of auxiliaries, and finite forms of the copula.

A root syllable is most likely to alliterate in a word of class A, less likely to alliterate in a word of class B, and quite unlikely to alliterate in a word of class C. Words of class A in Germanic languages usually have a strong phrasal stress, while words of class C usually undergo subordination. It seems reasonable to conclude, as Sievers did, that the probability of alliteration for a given syllable depends on its relative prominence within the phrase. Implicit in this view is the important claim that words in class B had phrasal stress intermediate between that characteristic of class A words and that characteristic of class C words.

The correspondence between relative prominence and word class is close, but not perfect. Under certain syntactic conditions (discussed in Chapter 9 below), the probability of alliteration for a word in a given class can change.

7.3 Positional Constraints on Alliterating Syllables

Another significant factor governing alliteration involves the position of the alliterating syllable within the line. Consider the following:

(43) (a) geongum ond ealdum, swylc him God sealde 72
to-young and to-old, what to-him God gave
"what God had given him to young and old"

(b) swylc him God sealde, geongum ond ealdum
what to-him God gave, to-young and to-old
"what God had given him to young and old"

(c) grim ond grædig, gearo sōna wæs 121
grim and greedy, ready at-once he-was
"grim and greedy, he was ready at once"

(d) *gearo sōna wæs, grim ond grædig
ready at-once he-was, grim and greedy
"he was ready at once, grim and greedy"

(e) *ealdum ond geongum, swylc him God sealde
to-old and to-young, what to-him God gave
"to old and young, what God had given him"

Reversal of the half-lines in (43a) produces (43b), which would have expressed in an acceptable way the idea that Hrothgar passed on to all what God had given him. Reversal of the half-lines in (43c) to produce (43d) would create no problems of sense or grammar, but would result in an unacceptable alliterative pattern. It is customary to describe this restriction by saying that only one syllable in the b-verse may alliterate, or that only one alliterating syllable may appear in the b-verse.[4] From a literal-minded point of view, of course, such expressions are meaningless: alliteration is an equivalence of at least two syllables, and no syllable may alliterate in isolation. Despite the imprecision, I will adopt the usual idiom on many occasions and speak as if alliteration were a property of individual syllables. This fiction makes it possible to discuss alliterative properties of half-lines in a somewhat less convoluted way. Linguists adopt a similar manner of speaking when they refer e.g. to "a syllable with secondary stress." A syllable never has secondary stress in isolation, but only in relation to other syllables of greater or lesser prominence.

Reversal of the first two adjectives in (43a) would not change the metrical pattern of the line, but would produce an unacceptable alliterative pattern (represented as (43e)). Metrists also employ an abbreviated form of speech to describe this feature of Old English alliteration, saying, for example, that in verses like *geongum ond ealdum* or *ealdum ond geongum* the first adjective alliterates obligatorily. The unacceptability of (43e) results from the fact that *geongum,* which alliterates with *God,* is the second rather than the first stressed word in the verse. The b-verse should "alliterate on *g-*" only in cases like (43a), when the first adjective in the a-verse also has *g-* alliteration. To sum up, then, we can say that in half-lines with two conjoined adjectives the first adjective alliterates obligatorily and the second adjective may alliterate only in the a-verse.

It would be difficult to explain these constraints in terms of stress subordination. Nothing in the history of Germanic languages would lead us to expect weak stress in the second of two conjoined adjectives.[5] Moreover, the requirement that a verse-initial word of class A must alliterate applies in the vast majority of cases, no matter what the syntax (cf. Sievers 1893, section 23.2).[6]

Kuryłowicz (1970, 16–20) suggests that the second foot of each verse undergoes a kind of *metrical subordination* to the first foot. According to Kuryłowicz, a syllable occupying a metrical position in a subordinated foot has a diminished probability of alliteration, like a syllable that undergoes stress subordination. This seems to me a valid insight, though as stated by Kuryłowicz it leaves many important facts unexplained. Within the framework proposed here, the principle of metrical subordination can be stated as a rule that determines the location of alliterating syllables in all verse types.

7.4 Linguistic Compounding

I shall argue below that the metrical subordination rule corresponds to the rule for stress in Old English compounds. First, however, a few linguistic preliminaries are in order. We must be quite clear about how linguistic compounding operates so that we can evaluate its relation to metrical compounding.

In Germanic languages, compounding is a binary operation that creates a larger word out of two smaller words (cf. Meid 1967, section 15). The unity of the larger word is marked by assignment of primary stress to the stressed syllable of the first constituent and by subordination of all other stressed syllables. The compound stress rule ignores many features of word structure, recognizing only the root syllables of the words being combined.

In the notational system employed by Liberman and Prince (1977), the Old English compound *sǣmannes* "sea-man's, sailor's" (g. sg.) would be represented by a tree structure like that below:

(44)

In (44), the root syllable *sǣ-* attaches to a node labeled *strong* and the root syllable *-man-* attaches to a node labeled *weak*. The strong and weak nodes are *dominated* by an unlabeled node above that represents the integrity of the whole constituent *sǣmannes*. Lines that connect higher nodes to lower nodes are called *branches,* and a node is said to *branch* if it dominates a strong-weak pair. The notational system does not provide a node for the inflectional *-es* of *sǣmannes* because such non-radical syllables play no role in determining compound stress (cf. Liberman and Prince 1977, 269). This means that all Old English compounds with two root syllables have identical stress trees. The diagram employed in (44) would also serve for bisyllabic forms like *sǣ-mann,* for "genitive compounds" like *Hrefna-wudu* "Ravenswood," and for compounds with a stressed prefix as the first constituent (e.g. *ed-wīt* "reproach," from the verb *ed-wītan* "to reproach").

The Liberman-Prince system allows for only two types of branching, strong-weak branching, like that in (44), and weak-strong branching.[7] If a node branches at all, it must branch into one strong node and one weak node. Applied to Old English compounding, this constraint captures the generalization that compound stress rules apply to two constituents at a time, increasing the prominence of the first relative to that of the second.[8]

Some Old English compounds have smaller compounds as subconstituents. Most often the smaller compound is a familiar "institutionalized" form that may have proceeded some way towards phonological lexicalization (cf. Bauer 1983, section 3.2.2). In the multiple compound *woruld-wīs-dōm,* for example, the second constituent is the familiar compound *wīs-dōm* "wise judgment," now lexicalized as *wisdom.* Forms like *woruldwīsdōm* are exceptional in that the smaller compound appears as the last constituent. Usually the smaller compound comes first, as in *Cant-wara-byrig* "Kent-dwellers'-city," now lexicalized as *Canterbury.*

Because it restricts branching so severely, the Liberman-Prince notation can represent compounds with three or more root syllables only through the device of embedding. The multiple compound *Cantwarabyrig* corresponds to the following diagram:

(45)

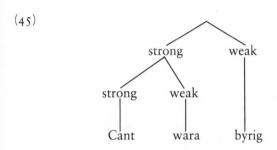

In isolation, *Cantwara* would correspond to a tree structure like that of (44), with an unlabeled node at the top. In (45), *Cantwara* is embedded as the first constituent of a larger compound, and the node dominating *Cant-* and *-wara-* is accordingly labeled strong. The representation in (45) makes an important claim about the relative stress of *-wara-* and *-byrig.* Whereas the weak node of *-byrig* is dominated by one node (the unlabeled node at the top), the weak node of *-wara-* is dominated by two nodes (the unlabeled node and the strong node representing *Cantwara*). The greater number of nodes above *-wara-* represents the fact that this constituent undergoes subordination twice, once in *Cantwara* and a second time in *Cantwarabyrig.* The constituent *byrig,* on the other hand, undergoes subordination only once, in *Cantwarabyrig.* Note that in the lexicalized form *Canterbury, -bury* retains stress on its root syllable and suffers relatively little change, whereas *-wara-* loses stress and undergoes reduction. In general, we seem to obtain the proper results for Old English multiple compounds by assuming that the compound stress rule applies in the same way at each level of structure, subordinating the second constituent to the first. This is, of course, the simplest assumption, the one we would make in the absence of contrary evidence.[9]

The relatively few multiple compounds attested in poetry behave as expected. Consider the following:

(46) (a)   edwīta / fela PPs 73.20
       of-reproaches many
       "many reproaches"

    (b)   hearm-edwīt / feala PPs 68.20
       injurious-reproach many
       "many an injurious reproach"

    (c)   þonne / edwīt-līf 2891b
       than reproach-life
       "than a life of shame"

Alliteration falls on the first syllable of *edwīta* in (46a) and on the first syllable of *hearm-edwīt* in (46b). Verse (46a) suggests that *ed-wīt* retained a perceptible degree of stress on its secondary constituent. If *-wīt-* has secondary or reduced stress, (46a) analyzes as the type E pattern Ssx/S, with resolution of the short syllable in *fela*. If *ed-wīta* had the stress pattern Sxx, on the other hand, the verse would represent the unmetrical pattern Sxx/S or an extremely unusual variant of Sxx/Sx with an unresolved syllable in the second foot.[10] Verse (46b) suggests that *-wīt* has reduced stress when subordinated twice in the multiple compound *hearm-edwīt* (cf. *-wara-* in *Cantwarabyrig*). On that hypothesis, the matching rules (2a-c) would allow *-wīt* to occupy an x position, and the verse would analyze as Ssx/S.

It seems unlikely that the metrical system would provide special foot patterns corresponding to the rare multiple compounds. If such patterns did exist, one would expect them to occupy second position obligatorily, like the complex patterns Sxs and Sxxs. Yet we do find verses like (46b). Here I will assume that the most weakly stressed root syllable in a multiple compound can mimic an unstressed, non-radical syllable in an ordinary compound with two roots.[11] The multiple compound *edwīt-līf,* with its smaller compound embedded as the first subconstituent, seems to represent the pattern Sxs in (46c). If so, rule (15a) should exclude forms

70

like *edwītlīf* from first position. I have not found any exceptional cases in the poetic corpus.

The multiple compounds attested in poetry alliterate on the root syllable of the first constituent, which would indicate that this syllable bore the most prominent stress. Old English multiple compounds would appear to differ from modern English constructions such as *second-floor balcony,* which are often regarded as compounds (e.g. in Bauer 1983, section 5.2.2), but which have the most prominent stress on the final constituent. One would not want to overestimate the strength of the metrical evidence, but it does seem consistent, as far as it goes, with the simplest view of multiple subordination in Old English.

7.5 Metrical Compounding

We are now in a position to formulate a rule for metrical subordination that mimics the behavior of the compound rule:

(47) When two constituents containing S positions appear within the same metrical domain, label the first constituent strong and the second constituent weak.

To see how (47) operates, consider a simple line consisting of two standard Sx/Sx verse patterns:

(48)

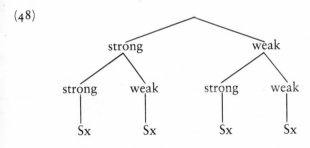

The tree diagram in (48) includes three levels of structure. An unlabeled node at the top corresponds to the metrical domain of the line. This node branches into two nodes representing the a-verse and b-verse. Since every verse contains at least one S, all a-verses will be strong and all b-verses will be weak. The verse nodes branch again into nodes representing feet. In this case, all four feet contain S positions, and the first foot in each verse is accordingly strong. The diagram in (48) conforms to the strict branching requirements imposed on stress trees. Each node that branches dominates exactly two constituents, one strong and the other weak. Note that only positions corresponding to root syllables are attached to nodes. There are no nodes for the x positions that correspond to non-radical syllables because, as we observed above, such constituents play no role in the higher-level rules that govern compounding and phrasal stress. This means that the verse patterns Sx/Sx, Sxx/Sx, S/Sxx, and Sx/Sxx have identical tree structures.

Lines with the strong-weak structure of (48) can have only two types of alliterative pattern:

(49) (a) mōdgan / mægnes, Metodes / hyldo 670
bold-one's might, Creator's grace
"the bold man's might and God's grace"

(b) wine / Scildinga, worold of- / lætest 1183
friend of-the-Scyldings, the-world may-leave
"you may die, friend of the Scyldings"

In lines like (49a-b), the S of the first foot and the S of the third foot must contain alliterating syllables. The S of the fourth foot may not contain an alliterating syllable. The S of the second foot may alliterate, as in (49a), but need not do so, as (49b) shows. The probability of alliteration for each S is directly related to its metrical prominence. The most prominent constituent is of course the S of the first foot, which never undergoes subordination, and which is not dominated by a weak node at any level of structure. Next in prominence is the first foot of the second half-line, which undergoes subordination once at the level of the line. The second and fourth feet both undergo subordination twice, once at the level of the verse and again at the level of the line. However, these two feet occupy different positions within the hierarchical tree structure: The second foot is the weak constituent of the strong verse, but the fourth foot is the weak constituent of the weak verse. We should not be surprised to find that the second foot has the greater prominence, as indicated by its compatibility with alliterating syllables.

We can specify the constraints on alliteration for all attested metrical patterns with the following rules:

(50) (a) The strongest two metrical positions within the line must contain alliterating syllables.

(b) A weak constituent of a weak constituent may not contain an alliterating syllable.

(c) No alliterating syllable may occupy an x position.

(d) Otherwise, alliteration is optional.[12]

Rules (47) and (50) apply to every type of line, respecting the foot boundaries and verse boundaries defined by our theory.

7.5.1 Metrical Compounding in Verses with Light Feet

Rule (47) determines strong-weak structure only when both constituents in a given domain contain S positions. When one constituent is inherently stronger than the other, (47) has no effect. Consider the following, for example:

(51)

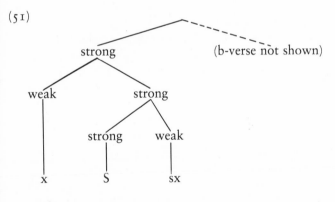

The diagram in (51) represents the hierarchical structure of an a-verse with the type C pattern x/Ssx. Within the second foot, we must provide a node for the s position, which corresponds to a root syllable. The relative strength of the two constituents in the foot is not affected by (47) because the rightmost constituent contains an s rather than an S. The s position, abstracted from the root syllable of a subordinated constituent, is by definition weaker than its accompanying S position.

In examples (49a-b), the feet are bound into verses by (47), the metrical equivalent of the compound rule. Through (47), phrases like *Metodes hyldo* become equivalent to large compounds like *middangeardes,* and must alliterate on the first constituent, as compounds do.[13] In (51), the x foot is bound to the following compound foot by the metrical equivalent of proclisis, which subordinates the root syllable of a function word in close syntactic composition with a following word of major category. Because light feet are abstracted from proclitics, they are subordinate, by their very nature, to a following foot containing an S position. Hence they must always be marked weak. As before, we provide nodes in (51) only for positions that correspond to root syllables. The first x of a light foot will attach to a node, since it represents the root syllable of a proclitic, but there will be no node for the second x of the xx foot, which represents a non-radical syllable. The hierarchical diagram of (51) would also serve for the patterns x/Sxs, x/Sxxs, xx/Ss, xx/Ssx, xx/Sxs, and xx/Sxxs: more generally, for the group of balanced patterns with a light foot in first position followed by a second foot with an S position and an s position.

When a balanced pattern appears as an a-verse, dominated by a strong node, the S position of the second foot will alliterate obligatorily, since this foot is not subordinated at any level and therefore has the greatest prominence (refer to (51) again). The following s node will be dominated by only one weak position, and may contain an optional alliterating syllable. When a balanced pattern appears as a b-verse, it comes under the domination of the weak node representing the second half-line:

(52)

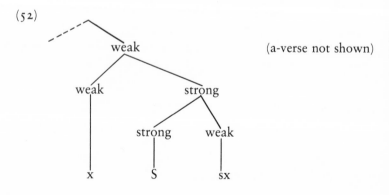

(a-verse not shown)

Here the S, subordinated once, is the second-most-prominent position in the line, and alliterates obligatorily. The following s position now lies within a weak constituent of a weak constituent, and cannot alliterate. In general, the embedding of a verse pattern under a weak node will limit its number of alliterating syllables to one. We do not need a special rule stating that the second half-line contains only one alliterating syllable.

Two verses of type C will illustrate the alliterative patterns possible in this group:

(53) (a)   wið / þēod-þrēaum 178a
           against people-distress
           "against a national calamity"

     (b)   in / gēar-dagum 1b   (alliteration on g-)
           in yore-days
           "in days of yore"

Example (53b) would be equally acceptable as an a-verse.

7.5.2 *Metrical Compounding in Heavy Verses*

We now consider the hierarchical structure of heavy verses with a compound pattern in the second foot (S/Ssx, S/Sxs, S/Sxxs, Sx/Ss, Sx/Ssx, Sx/Sxs, Sx/Sxxs, and Sxx/Ss). An a-verse pattern of the form S/Ssx (type Da) can serve as a representative example:

(54)

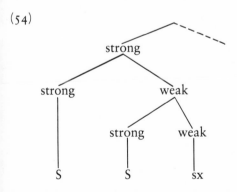

Here both feet contain an S position. Accordingly, (47) applies at the level of the verse, marking the first foot strong and the second foot weak. In the pattern of (51), the s position of the second foot is dominated by only one weak node, and may therefore alliterate at the poet's option. In (54), the s position of the second foot lies within the weak constituent of a weak constituent, and cannot alliterate. Alliteration is optional for the immediately preceding S position (which is dominated by a single weak node) and obligatory for the S position of the first foot (which remains unsubordinated). When verses with this hierarchical structure occur in the second half-line, the S of the second foot comes under the domination of a second weak node, and the possibility of double alliteration is removed. Alliteration remains obligatory for the S of the first foot, which would be subordinated once in the second half-line. The following verses display the alliterative patterns compatible with (54):

(55) (a)   lēof / lēod-cyning 54a
        dear people-king
        "the dear king of the people"

    (b)   fēond / man-cynnes 164b   (alliteration on f-)
        enemy of-mankind
        "enemy of mankind"

Example (55b) would also qualify as an a-verse.

7.5.3 Metrical Compounding in Reversed Patterns

Some interesting complications arise when we consider the hierarchical structure of reversed patterns (Ssx/S and Ss/Sx). An a-verse pattern of type E will serve as an example:

(56)

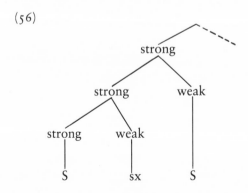

In reversed patterns, alliteration is obligatory on the leftmost S, the strongest metrical position. As with other heavy patterns, reversed patterns occupying the first half-line may alliterate on the S position of the second foot. Note, however, the important difference between stress tree (56) and stress tree (54). In (54) the s position attaches to a weak node dominated by the weak node of the second foot. In (56) the s position attaches to a weak node dominated by the strong node of the first foot. Since the s of (56) is dominated by only one weak node, we would expect to find some verses with two alliterating syllables in the first foot. These do in fact occur:

(57) (a) Gūð-Gēata / lēod 1538a
       War-Geats' prince
       "Prince of the War-Geats"

    (b) swutol sang / scopes 90a
       clear song of-the-poet
       "clear song of the poet"

    (c) beorht bēacen / Godes 570a
       bright beacon of-God
       "bright beacon of God"

    (d) syn-snǣdum / swealh 743a
       in-great-gulps gobbled
       "gobbled in great gulps"

The syntactic structures of (57a-d) leave no doubt about the proper location of the foot boundary (cf. (3–5)). These must be regarded as examples of reversed patterns with double alliteration in the first foot. The metrical subordination rule attains its full generality in (57d), which has three alliterating syllables.

    Examples (57a-d) are worth considering in some detail because they provide strong evidence against Sievers's system of verse division. The theory proposed here resembles that of Pope (1942) and Creed (1966) in allowing for two alliterating syllables within the foot. Sievers, on the other hand, allows alliterative patterns to dictate foot structure, assigning each alliterating syllable to a foot of its own. I pointed out above (section 1.5.2) that Sievers goes against his own syntactic rationale for division of heavy verses when he divides types B and C. To preserve the one-to-one correspondence between feet and alliterating syllables, one would also have to divide the heavy verses (57a-c) against the syntax. Sievers (1893, section 23.3) shows his awareness of the problem when he discusses (57c) and a related Old Saxon verse *(Heliand* 412a). In such verses, we are told, the last two words form a kind of quasi-compound: we must translate *beorht bēacen Godes* as "fair God's-beacon." Sievers offers no independent evidence to support this implausible explanation, and its futility is clearly demonstrated by (57a) and (57d), which should have been discussed in the same context, but were simply swept under the rug.

One cannot account for (57a-d) plausibly as errors of the scribe or the poet. Compound patterns occupy second position in most cases, and irregular alliteration on an s position would therefore tend to occur most often in the structure represented by (54), if it occurred at all. Recall too that the poet takes special pains to restrict metrical complexity in reversed patterns (cf. (15a-b), (21a)). A poet so sensitive to causes of analytical effort in verses of this type would hardly overlook a flagrant violation of the alliterative rules. We should regard (57a-d) as acceptable.

We must now explain, of course, why verses like (57a-d) occur so seldom. The low frequency of verses like (57a) and (57d) is attributable to the low frequency of compounds with two alliterating syllables. Only eighteen verses in *Beowulf* contain such compounds, including (57a) and (57d).[14] Verses like (57b-c) have a low frequency because the poet avoids word groups in the first foot of reversed patterns. Examples (57b-c) are two of only nine such a-verses.[15] Feet consisting of word groups are of course more difficult to perceive than are those occupied by a single word, so the avoidance of word groups in the first foot of reversed patterns comes as no surprise. When we take all these factors into account, the number of verses like (57a-d) seems about as expected. Observe too that the s of the first foot in (56), though eligible for alliteration, is metrically weaker than the S of the second foot (cf. *-wara-* in (45) once again). In view of the direct link between metrical prominence and alliteration, we would expect the poet to place an optional alliterating syllable most often on the stronger of two available positions. Hence the relatively higher frequency of verses like the following:

(58) sinc-fāge / sel 167a
      treasure-adorned hall
      "hall adorned with treasure"
      [Ssx/S]

We can conclude that the rarity of double alliteration in the first foot is a secondary consequence of the rarity of verses with certain linguistic features. We need not (and therefore *should* not) complicate the alliterative rules to explain the oddness of verses like (57a-d).

7.5.4 Peculiarities of Verses with an Ss Foot

The following types of xx/Ss verse patterns with double alliteration are unattested:

(59) (a) *ond on ge- / flit fōr (cf. 865a)
          and in a-race went
          "and went racing"

     (b) *oþþe se / brȳd-būr (cf. 921a)
          or the woman-bower
          "or the women's bower"

Examples (59a-b) have the hierarchical structure of (51), which permits double alliteration in the a-verse. However, xx/Ss is the rarest member of its set.[16] For verses of such complexity, word groups seem to be ruled out altogether in the second foot (cf. (33)). The unacceptability of (59a) has to do with its foot structure, not with its pattern of alliterating syllables. The absence of verses like (59b) can be attributed to the restricted frequency of compounds with double alliteration. We would not expect to find these rare compounds in such a small group of examples.

The extremely heavy pattern Ss/Ss is even rarer than the pattern xx/Ss.[17] As with other complex types, Ss/Ss occurs only in the first half-line:

(60)

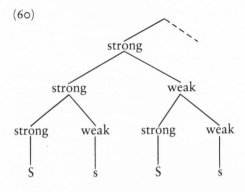

Alliteration is theoretically possible on the s of the first foot, which is dominated by only one weak node. However, we would normally expect the poet to place an optional alliterating syllable on the stronger of the two possible locations, the S of the second foot (cf. (58)). A handful of Ss/Ss verses would not be expected to include the more complex alternative (and do not).

7.5.5 *Alliteration in Light Verses*

The last hierarchical structure to be considered is that corresponding to verses with a single S position and no s position (x/Sxx, xx/Sx, xx/Sxx). An a-verse pattern of type A3 (xx/Sx) would have the following tree diagram:

(61)

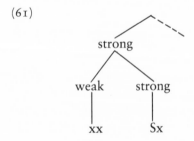

Here again the light foot, the metrical equivalent of a proclitic, is subordinate to the foot that contains the S. The alliterating syllable occupies the only possible location, the S position of the second foot. On the exclusion of the pattern xx/Sx from the second half-line, see section 5.3.

7.6 Implications

Work on metrical problems by theoretical linguists is often inspired by the hope of discovering information about underlying phonological structure unattainable from any other source (see especially Kiparsky 1968, 1972). Old English alliterative patterns appear to provide such information. We have seen that rule (47) applies to metrical patterns with two S positions just as the compounding rule applies to compound words with two root syllables. Yet rule (47) also applies to metrical patterns that have few analogues in ordinary speech. The hierarchical structure of (48), which has four S positions, corresponds to a compound with four root syllables. No such compounds appear in the surviving records of Old English, though the competence of the Old English speaker would have allowed for their creation (cf. Bauer 1983, section 4.2.2.1). Problems in the study of multiple subordination sometimes arise even when we have access to native speakers who will supply the desired forms. Liberman and Prince (1977) note the possibility "that details of the relationship between nonprimary stresses in long words would shed direct empirical light on the geometry of word trees," but they caution that this relationship is rather unstable and heavily influenced by rhythmic factors (p. 269). It is difficult to distinguish, say, between the weak constituent of a weak constituent and the weak constituent of a strong constituent because such subtle distinctions in relative prominence may be neutralized in actual pronunciation. This kind of problem has motivated a theory of phonological "grids" derived from stress trees but suppressing certain features of tree structure (see the recent discussion in Hayes 1984).[18] For those interested in the underlying phonological structure of Old English compounds, alliterative patterns may provide evidence of a quality that would be difficult to match even if native speakers were available. The alliterative rules (50a-d) operate directly on trees created by (47), and are sensitive to the most subtle features of arboreal geometry. Rhythmic factors cannot distort these patterns of relative prominence because the rules for alliteration apply to abstract metrical positions rather than to actual syllables.

The alliterative rules also provide a particularly clear insight into higher-level organization of metrical patterns. Assignment of foot nodes to higher nodes in work on iambic pentameter is based on somewhat problematic indications, such as the position of the caesura (see Kiparsky 1977, 227–30). In Old English poetry, the well-defined binary structure of the verse and the line imposes rigid constraints on the location of higher-level nodes, and the stress trees we posit can be tested against the rich evidence of alliterative patterning. The results provide a new kind of support for the claim that tree structures play a crucial role in the study of poetic meter (cf. Kiparsky 1977, 190–1).

8

METRICAL SUBORDINATION WITHIN THE FOOT

8.1 Double Alliteration in the First Half-line

We have now explained the constraints on alliteration observed by Sievers (1885, 1893), identifying the positions of obligatory alliteration and the positions compatible with optional alliteration. However, we must still deal with some important constraints brought to light since Sievers wrote. Bliss (1958) noticed that double alliteration is obligatory in certain types of heavy verses which therefore never appear in the second half-line. Bliss also discovered a strong stylistic preference for double alliteration in certain variants of the standard pattern Sx/Sx. As it turns out, the framework employed here can provide natural explanations for these findings.

Let us first consider the incidence of double alliteration in standard patterns:

(62) (a)   lange / þrāge 114a
         a-long time
         "for a long time"

    (b)   sinc æt / symle 81a
         treasure at feasting
         "treasure at the feast"

    (c)   folce / (tō) frōfre 14a
         to-people as consolation
         "as a consolation to the people"

Only about 29% of a-verses like (62a) have double alliteration, but in verses like (62b-c) the figure rises to 93% (cf. Bliss 1958,

section 43). I would relate the preference for double alliteration in
(62b-c) to the relatively greater complexity of these patterns. Note
that the variant represented by (62a) has the simplest imaginable
structure, with each foot occupied by a trochaic word. In such
cases, linguistic material expresses the standard metrical pattern
directly, and the audience needs no further assistance. When a
word group occupies the first foot, however, as in (62b), or when
extrametrical words are present, as in (62c), a second alliterating
syllable facilitates recovery of the underlying pattern by marking
the leftward boundary of the second foot. Kuryłowicz (1975, 151)
emphasizes the importance of obligatory alliteration as a *Grenzsignal* (boundary marker) for the line. The optional alliterative
element seems to serve as a verse-internal *Grenzsignal*.

8.2 Categorical Restrictions on Alliteration in Heavy Verses

The higher frequency of double alliteration in verses like (62b-c)
indicates a stylistic preference rather than any sort of categorical
rule. There are many verses like (62b-c) in the second half-line,
and the corresponding variants with single alliteration in the first
half-line occur too often to ignore. In certain heavy verse types, on
the other hand, double alliteration seems genuinely obligatory:

(63) (a) bēagas / (ond) brād gold 3105a[1]
      rings and ample gold
      "rings and much gold"

   (b) bær / (on) bearm scipes 896a[2]
      bore into bosom of-the-ship
      "carried into the ship's interior"

   (c) þrȳðlīc / þegna hēap 400a[3]
      splended thanes' troop
      "splendid troop of thanes"

   (d) (Ā-)rīs, / rīces weard 1390a
      Arise, kingdom's guardian
      "Arise, guardian of the kingdom"

   (e) Godes yrre / bær 711b[4]
      God's wrath he-bore
      "He endured God's wrath"

(f)   sunu dēoð / wrecan 1278b
      son's death to-avenge
      "to avenge the son's death"

Metrical rules independent of alliteration determine the location
of foot boundaries in these verses. All must conform to (3b),
which requires that the foot boundary coincide with the major
constituent break. Verses (63a-b) must also conform to (15a),
which rules out a foot of the form Sxs or Sxxs in first position.
Single alliteration occurs when two words of class A occupy the
first foot, as in (63e-f). When two such words occupy the second
foot, as in (63a-d), the S position of that foot must contain an
alliterating syllable. As a result, the syntactic structures represented by (63a-d) appear only as a-verses.

The account of heavy verses in Bliss (1958, sections 76–83)
does not distinguish systematically between verses like (63a-d)
and verses like the following, which do not always have double
alliteration:

(64) (a)   secg / weorce gefeh 1569b[5]
           man at-work rejoiced
           "the man rejoiced in his work"

     (b)   hond / rond gefēng 2609b[6]
           hand shield grasped
           "his hand grasped his shield"

     (c)   holm / heolfre wēoll 2138a[7]
           water with-blood welled
           "the water was turbulent with blood"

In (64a-c), the major constituent break comes between the first
word and the second, and the foot boundary must appear in that
location according to (3b). Hence (64a) analyzes as S/Sxxs and
(64b-c) analyze as S/Sxs. When double alliteration occurs, as in
(64c), the second alliterating syllable occupies the S of the second
foot, as we would expect (cf. (54)). Now in (63a-d), the s position
of the second foot is occupied by the root syllable of a class A
word. In (64a-c), on the other hand, the s position is occupied by
the root syllable of a class B word. It seems that double allitera-

tion becomes obligatory only when the syllable occupying the s position of the second foot has prominent sentence stress.

A few variants like the following also appear as b-verses with single alliteration:

(65) (a)   strēam / ūt þonan 2545b
           stream out thence
           "a stream from out of there"

    (b)   Sinc / ēaðe mæg 2764b[8]
           treasure easily may
           "treasure may easily"

The syntactic constituency of adverbs is notoriously problematic, but most would agree, I think, that the major constituent break falls between the first word and the second in (65a-b). In these verses, the third word is a particle or auxiliary of class C that acquires a weak stress when removed from proclitic position. Here again the absence of double alliteration coincides with occupation of the s position by a syllable with relatively low prominence.

8.3 Metrical Compounding of Small Feet into Larger Feet

We can explain the distribution of heavy verses with double alliteration by assigning a new role to (47), the metrical equivalent of the compound stress rule. In Old English, compounding creates larger words out of smaller words, assigning prominence to the first constituent word. Let us assume that (47) can create a larger foot out of two smaller feet by assigning metrical prominence (and alliteration) to the first constituent foot. This theoretical maneuver may seem rather bizarre at first, but it allows us to simplify the rule system and helps, as we shall see later, to explain the structure of hypermetrical verses.

The labeling rule (2a) normally requires a syllable of primary stress to occupy an S position, but makes an exception for verses like (63a-f). By eliminating the exception, we obtain the simpler rule below:

(66)   A syllable of primary stress must occupy an S position.

Rule (66) explains the absence of verses like the following:

86

(67)   *þrȳ∂līc / secga / hēap (cf. (63c))
       splendid men's troop
       "splendid troop of men"

The unmetrical (67) contains three class A words with primary stress on the root syllable. In a system with the revised rule (66), (67) analyzes obligatorily as Sx/Sx/S, violating rule II, which defines a verse as a pair of feet.

We must now account, of course, for the presence of verses like those in (63), which will also contain three S positions. To do so, we add the following refinements to (47):

(68) (a)   Assignment of metrical stress to the first constituent of a small foot pair creates a higher-level foot.

     (b)   A constituent receiving metrical stress must contain an alliterating syllable.

As formulated in section 2.3, the overlap constraint (12) rules out foot pairs that overlap larger feet, with the systematic exceptions noted in our discussion of hypermetrical verses (Chapter 6). This would leave no room for small pairs such as S/S, S/Sx, and Sx/S, which overlap the foot patterns Ss, Ssx, and Sxs, respectively. Our new rule (68a) can render foot pairs like S/S, S/Sx, and Sx/S equivalent to the compound feet they overlap. If the first S in, say, S/Sx receives metrical stress by (47), that foot pair can masquerade as an Ssx foot. The second S in the S/Sx pair will retain its identity as an S position, however, and can thus accommodate the root syllable of a class A word. In view of the close relationship between stress and alliteration, it seems natural to view assignment of metrical stress as assignment of alliteration. A glance at the tree structures in Chapter 7 will show that any constituent assigned prominence by (47) will contain an alliterating syllable. Rule (68b) now requires alliteration on the first S of any metrical domain containing more than one S, whether it be a line, a verse, or a foot.

We can use tree notation to represent the hierarchical structure of verses with embedded foot pairs. The following diagram corresponds to (63c):

(69)

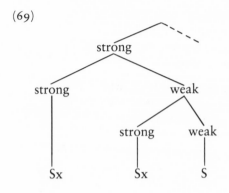

Diagram (69) bears a close resemblance to (54), but in (69) the lowest-level weak node dominates an S rather than an s. Since both constituents of the second foot contain S positions, (47) applies, marking the first S strong. By rule (68b), this strong S must alliterate. As (47) applies, it creates a higher-level foot, represented here by a weak node dominating the last two S positions. The strong node representing the a-verse now branches into two feet, as required by rule II and the general constraints on tree structure. Application of (47) at the level of the verse makes alliteration obligatory on the S of the first foot as well. The final S, dominated by two weak nodes, may not contain an alliterating syllable. We can represent the structure of (69) in abbreviated notation as Sx// Sx/S, where the double slash indicates the boundary of the higher-level foot.

The unmetrical verse (67) corresponds to an ill-formed tree structure like that below:

(70)

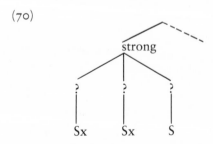

The lack of alliteration on the medial S of (67) shows that this position has not received metrical stress (cf. (68b)). The verse-final

S remains unsubordinated, and no higher-level foot node is created. Under these conditions, the strong node representing the a-verse branches directly into three feet, violating rule II and the general constraints on tree structures. Violation of rule II and violation of branching constraints seem to go hand in hand. There may be a deep connection between use of alliteration, which coincides with metrical compounding, and the binary structure of Old English metrical patterns.

In (64a-c) and (65a-b) the words in verse-final position have weak stress rather than strong stress, and their root syllables may therefore occupy s positions, mimicking the subordinated root syllables in compounds like *middangeard* and *mancynnes*. Verses like those in (64) and (65) have the hierarchical structure of (54). In this structure, the second foot contains only one S position, and (47) will not apply. An optional alliterating syllable may occupy the S of the second foot (cf. (55a), (64c)), but need not do so (cf. (55b), (64a-b), (65a-b)).

One might imagine a somewhat less exotic account of double alliteration employing the concept of the *Grenzsignal*. We could speculate, for example, that the poet used double alliteration when the stress contour of the verse gave no hint about verse division. Verses like (63e-f) show, however, that the less exotic theory leaves several facts unexplained. Verses (63e) and (64b) both have two strongly stressed constituents followed by a weakly stressed constituent, but the poet provides no *Grenzsignal* to indicate the difference in metrical structure, and the audience must use syntactic cues to determine the location of the foot boundary. Verse (63f) contains three words of class A, like (63a-d), but the poet does not supply a *Grenzsignal* on the last S to indicate that the foot boundary falls after the second word. One cannot dismiss examples like (63e-f), which represent a considerable proportion of the complex reversed patterns with a word group in the first foot. Here, if anywhere, a *Grenzsignal* would be obligatory. Note too the presence of a few verses like (57a-d), in which the second alliterating element would actually tend to mislead the audience about the location of the foot boundary. In discussing the type A1 verses of (62), we noted that the preference for double alliteration in the more complex variants was too weak to block a few instances with single alliteration in the a-verse or to exclude such variants from the second half-line. In heavier patterns, we also find a preference for a verse-internal *Grenzsignal* (cf. Bliss 1958, section 76); but this preference is not strong enough to rule out b-verses like (63e-f) or a-verses like (57a-d). The only categorical constraints are those imposed by (47), (50), and (68).

Verse (63f) would correspond to the following hierarchical structure:

(71)

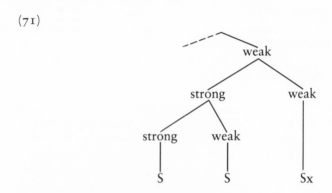

Here (47) applies to the first two S nodes and renders them equivalent to Ss. Using abbreviated notation, we can represent the structure of (71) as S/S//Sx. In this instance, the higher-level foot node dominating the smaller foot pair stands first, and is accordingly strong. Since only the first S alliterates obligatorily, (63f) may appear as a b-verse. The hierarchical structure represented in (71) also corresponds to the pattern S/Sx//S of (63e). The structure corresponding to a-verses like (57b-c) will have a verse node labeled strong, but will be identical to (71) in all other respects.

Our new rules allow substitution of S for s in most of the structures discussed above (Chapter 7). The substitution adds to complexity, however, and is restricted or forbidden in certain patterns that are already complex (cf. (59a-b) and accompanying discussion). Substitution of S for s occurs most often in the relatively simple balanced patterns x/Ssx and x/Sxs, which now have variants of the form x//S/Sx and x//Sx/S, respectively. Our commitment to rule (66) requires us to analyze (28a), for example, as x//S/Sx rather than as x/Ssx. Verse (31) provides an example of what we now regard as an x//Sx/S pattern. In all such variants, the first S of the higher-level foot must alliterate in accordance with (68b).

8.4 Word Groups and Genitive Compounds

Our more restrictive theory isolates a verse regarded as unmetrical by Bliss (1958, section 87):

(72) seah / (on) enta geweorc 2717b
      he-looked on giants' work
      "he looked at the work (or edifice) of the giants"

Word division in (72) reflects standard editorial practice. The verb *seah* alliterates, and the second foot appears to contain a heavy word group. If *geweorc* has primary stress, rule (66) will force analysis of (72) as S/(x)Sxx/S, an illegal three-foot pattern (cf. (67)). One cannot plausibly attribute (72) to scribal error because of a striking parallel in *The Ruin:*

(73) brosnað / enta geweorc 2b
      decays giants'-work
      "the work (or edifice) of the giants decays"

Here again the assumption that *geweorc* is a class A word implies an unacceptable pattern, in this case Sx/Sxx/S. From the perspective of our theory, then, the problem is quite sharply defined. The string *enta geweorc*, which seems analogous to *secga hēap* in (67), occurs where we would expect a compound word or a word group like *weorce gefeh* (cf. (64a)). If we could somehow show that *geweorc* had undergone stress subordination, we could analyze (72) as S/(x)Sxxs, a type Db pattern compatible with single alliteration (see (54) for the relevant hierarchical structure).

I would argue that *enta geweorc* is in fact a genitive compound *entageweorc*, with subordination of the final constituent. On this hypothesis, *entageweorc* could occupy an Sxxs foot. The failure to identify *entageweorc* as a genitive compound is quite understandable. As we noted above in section 1.1.2, genitive compounds have a morphology and spelling identical to that of word groups.

A genitive compound becomes recognizable only when it undergoes semantic specialization to the extent that the meaning of the
whole is no longer predictable from the meaning of the parts. The
genitive compound *Hrefnawudu,* for example, refers to a particular place called "Ravenswood," not to any forested area that happens to include a rookery. In many cases, the semantic evidence
will be difficult to evaluate, and lexicographers may not agree.
The form *dōmesdæg* appears as a compound in Clark Hall and
Meritt (1969, supplement), but Campbell (1972, v) rejects such a
form because he finds no decisive evidence of specialization in the
Old English data. Evidently Campbell views the restricted sense
evident in Modern English *doomsday* as a later development.

In early Germanic languages, genitive compounding was restricted to just a few semantic types (see Meid 1967, sections 17–
19). There were plant names like OHG *hanen-zunga* "Roost-
er's-tongue"; characterizations of persons like OE *landes-mann*
"inhabitant of a country, native"; and names of dwellings or archi-
tectural components like Gothic *baurgs-waddjus* "city wall," OE
nunnan-mynster "nun's cloister, nunnery." No one seems to have
noticed that *entageweorc* qualifies as a member of the third class.
Wherever *entageweorc* appears, it refers to an ancient ruin of im-
pressive stone construction, indicating a considerable degree of semantic specialization. If we take *-geweorc* in its well-attested sense
of "edifice," we obtain a compound meaning "old edifice of the
giants" with a semantic structure like that of *nunnan-mynster.* It is
interesting to note that the *entageweorc* is distinguished from other
artifacts of gigantic provenance. An ancient paved road or venera-
ble sword does not evoke the formula *eald entageweorc,* but appears as *enta ærgeweorc* "long-ago work of the giants."[9] In this
phrase, *enta* and *geweorc* are separated, and *geweorc* has its full
range of meanings. To appreciate the naturalness of *entageweorc* as
a specialized technical expression, compare the archaeological term
cyclopean, which refers to stone buildings of ancient Mycenaean
workmanship (OED, s.v.).

8.5 Poetic Compounds and Word Groups

Verses like the following suggest that our theory is still not sufficiently restrictive:

(74) (a)   biter ond / beadu-scearp 2704a
           sharp and battle-keen
           "of warlike sharpness"

    (b)   brond / (nē) beado-mēcas 1454a
           brand nor battle-swords
           "no brand nor warlike swords"

    (c)   brogdne / beadu-sercean 2755a
           braided battle-mail
           "warlike mailcoat of linked rings"

    (d)   (ge-)wēold / wīg-sigor 1554a
           determined war-victory
           "brought about the victory"

    (e)   heal-ærna / mǣst 78a
           of-hall-halls greatest
           "greatest of halls"

    (f)   gūð-rinc / monig 838b
           battle-warrior many
           "many a warlike fighter"

These correspond to (63a-f) except that the heavy foot contains a poetic compound rather than a word group. In verses like (74a-d), double alliteration appears to be obligatory (cf. (63a-d)). In verses like (74e-f), single alliteration may occur (cf. (63e-f)). It seems that poetic compounds obey constraints identical to those governing heavy word groups.

By "poetic compound" I refer to a form with a semantic structure unlike that of ordinary compounds. In the most common poetic compounds, the first constituent, or *combinative*, stands in a pleonastic relation to the second constituent, or *base*, without restricting its meaning (cf. Meid 1967, section 30).[10] By interchanging the redundant combinatives, the poet employs the base under varying metrical conditions.

Combinatives frequently allude to heroic activities like drinking (e.g. *medo-* in *medo-heall* "mead-hall"). The narrative makes it quite clear that a "mead-hall" was a general-purpose building rather than a tavern. Drinking was common enough in this type of edifice, but it also served as a dormitory, and was in no way distinct from what the poet refers to elsewhere simply as a "hall" *(heall)*. A substantial proportion of combinatives comes from a small class of lexical items with the sense of "war" or "warlike" (cf. Klaeber 1950, lxiv). The combinative *gūð-* employed in (74f) provides the first constituent for 29 other poetic forms, some of them used more than once. Of comparable productivity are *wæl-* (24 different compounds), *hilde-* (25), *heaðo-* (20), *wīg-* (16), *here-* (14), and *beadu-* (12). When these appear with words referring to military equipment, as often happens, they create a striking effect of redundancy. The base *bill* "sword," for example, appears in *gūð-bill* "war-sword" (803a, 2584b); *hilde-bill* "battle-sword" (557a, 1520a, 1666b, 2679a); and *wīg-bill* "combat-sword" (1607a). In view of the fact that swords exist only for fighting, such heroic terms can denote nothing more than "sword." Several poetic compounds appear in more than one poem, which would indicate that poets inherited them whole, along with other devices of traditional diction. However, the large number of unique occurrences in *Beowulf* suggests that poets typically coined such compounds as the opportunity to employ them arose (cf. Brodeur 1959, 6–11).

The less common type of poetic compound called a *kenning* has a characteristic metaphorical structure. The motivation for compound kennings seems to be in part metrical (cf. Magoun 1953), though they must have cost more effort to create than did pleonastic compounds. In verse 10, for example, we find the kenning *hron-rād* "whale-road, road of the whale" employed as a designation for the sea.[11] By replacing *hron-* with other combinatives, the poet obtains two synonymous kennings alliterating on *s-*, *swan-rād* "swan-road" (200a) and *segl-rād* "sail-road" (1429b).

Poetic compounds facilitate composition not just because they provide alliteration but also because they fill out the metrical pattern. Expressions like *swan-rād* did not arise because the poet lacked a word for "sea" with the proper alliteration: the ordinary word for "sea" in Old English is *sǣ*. Forms like *swan-rād* are useful because *ofer swan-rāde* (200a) constitutes an acceptable verse and **ofer sǣ* does not. The poetic compound also has a purely aesthetic dimension. Perhaps the most characteristic feature of Old English verse is a marked preference for varied expression that goes far beyond the coining of useful synonyms (cf. Russom 1978). Many have noticed the usefulness of poetic compounds, but no one seems to appreciate the force of the rule requiring them to alliterate, which imposes severe constraints on their employment as verse-fillers or as rhetorical alternatives. Formulas like *lēof land-fruma* (31a) "beloved nation-king" have variants like *lēof lēod-cyning* (54a) "beloved people-king," but no variants like **lēof þēod-cyning*. This last expression has the right meaning but the wrong alliterative pattern.

Not all compounds restricted to poetry are true poetic compounds. Consider the following verse, in which the compound fails to alliterate:

(75) hroden / ealo-wǣge 495b (alliteration on *h-*)
      decorated ale-cup
      "the decorated ale-cup"

The traditional diction of Old English poetry handed down many simplex words no longer used in prose. Old English *wǣge* "cup" occurs only in poetry, and the archaic character of this simplex explains sufficiently why *ealo-wǣge*, which contains *wǣge* as a secondary constituent, fails to appear in prose. Semantically, *ealo-wǣge* differs from true poetic compounds, corresponding to ordinary forms like Modern English *beer mug* rather than to forms like *medo-heall* "mead hall."[12] Alliteration is obligatory only for compounds with deviant semantics.

In section 1.1.2 we noted that compounds entering the language behave at first like two words in most respects. Only later, after the process of lexicalization has had time to work, does a compound come to resemble simplex words. As a nonce form, the typical poetic compound would obviously not undergo lexicalization to any significant extent. Lexicalization would occur only if the poetic compound entered ordinary language for some reason.[13]

These considerations motivate a rule of the following form:

(76) Poetic compounds count as two words.[14]

By (76), a noun or adjective occurring as the secondary constituent of a poetic compound will be regarded as equivalent to an unsubordinated noun or adjective, which must occupy an S position. Like the heavy word groups of (63), the poetic compounds of (74) will alliterate obligatorily.

The equivalence relation between poetic compounds and heavy word groups has some implications for current thinking about stress subordination. Chomsky and Halle (1968, 26 n. 15) suggest that "what the phonetician 'hears' in utterances depends very heavily on internalized rules that predict perceived phonetic shape." On this hypothesis, what we call "secondary stress" is recognizable as such not just because its acoustic realization differs from that of primary stress, but also because the hearer knows that the root syllable in question lies within the secondary constituent of a normal compound form. The anomalous semantic properties of poetic compounds may have interfered with recognition of the stress in their secondary constituents even if this stress was identical acoustically to that of the secondary constituents in ordinary compounds. A stressed syllable not perceptibly subordinated would naturally obey the restrictions placed on syllables with primary stress. It is interesting to note that pleonastic compounds reverse the relative semantic prominence characteristic of ordinary compounds, in which the first constituent marks an important distinction. In pleonastic compounds, the second constituent carries the whole referential burden, and the first constituent is semantically inessential. Perhaps the semantic prominence of the second constituent translates into perceived phonological prominence.

8.6 Editorial Misunderstanding of Poetic Compounds

The view of artificial compounds advanced here rules out some editorial conjectures about difficult verses. Klaeber, for example, emends *hwate Scildingas* "the bold Scyldings" (3005b) to *hwate scild-wigan* "the bold shield-warriors." The term *scild-wiga* appears otherwise only in *Beowulf* 288a (spelled as *scyld-wiga*). Its redundancy marks it as a poetic compound, one of several in which the name of a military implement serves as a combinative for the base *wiga* "warrior" (cf. *æsc-wiga, byrn-wiga, gār-wiga, lind-wiga, rand-wiga*). These expressions do not refer to distinct categories of fighting men: all have the denotation "warrior." As an artificial compound, *scild-wiga* must alliterate. Klaeber's conjectural **hwate scild-wigan*, which alliterates on *h-*, violates the meter.

Our theory also makes a distinction, sometimes disregarded by editors, between two types of proper name. Consider the forms

Gūð-Scilfingas and *Heaðo-Scilfingas,* derived by adding the familiar combinatives *gūð-* and *heaðo-* to the base *Scilfingas.* The compound forms are not attested as genuine tribal names, and the poet uses them interchangeably with the tribal name *Scilfingas.* Many artificial names similar to *Gūð-Scilfingas* appear in *Beowulf,* and they always alliterate on the first constituent, like other poetic compounds. Sometimes, however, compound formations typical of heroic verse find their way into ordinary speech. *Heaðo-Beardan* bears a close resemblance to *Heaðo-Scilfingas,* but we know that the former served as a genuine tribal name because the people who feuded with King Hrothgar appear as *Heaðo-Beardan* in the poetic list of tribes and kings called *Widsith* (cf. Klaeber 1950, xxxiv-xv). The Heathobards were not simply "Bards," but constituted a distinct group, differing, for example, from the Langobards (see Chambers 1967, 23). As a specialized proper name, *Heaðo-Beardan* would have undergone stress subordination within its second constituent, and could have escaped the constraint that governs poetic compounds. In fact, it has done so: In *Beowulf* 2032b, g. pl. *Heaðo-Beardna* occupies the last foot of the b-verse, and does not alliterate. Evidently compound tribal names could appear in poetry without alliterating, but only if they had currency in ordinary speech.

At line 445a, the manuscript reads *mægen hreð manna,* which has been interpreted as "power-glory of men" and alternatively as "power of the Glory-men." The latter interpretation posits a compound proper name form *Hreð-manna* that alliterates on the secondary constituent but not on the primary constituent. Elsewhere in *Beowulf,* the secondary constituent of a compound alliterates only if the preceding constituent alliterates also.[15] Klaeber and Dobbie recognize this difficulty, but print *mægen Hreð-manna* in their editions nevertheless. According to Dobbie (1953, 139), "it is tempting to find a tribal name in this line, as a variation of *Geotena leode.*" Now the ordinary name of the tribe in question is *Gēatas,* and *Hreð-men* is not recorded elsewhere in historical materials. A form *Hreð-manna* would therefore appear to be a poetic compound. Yet the fact that *Hreð-manna* does not alliterate on *H-* shows that it cannot be a poetic compound. The alliterative pattern of *mægen Hreð-manna* is suspect not just in one way but in two.[16]

8.7 Alliteration in Hypermetrical Verses

The rules for alliteration seem to apply within hypermetrical patterns exactly as they do within normal patterns. Consider the following a-verses, for example:

(77) (a) bēagas // (ond) brād / gold 3105a
 rings and ample gold
 "rings and much gold"

    (b) landes // (ond) locenra / bēaga 2995a
 of-land and of-linked rings
 "of land and linked rings"

In (77a), cited earlier as (63a), double alliteration is obligatory because of the heavy word group occupying the second foot. The same constraint applies to the hypermetrical (77b), where the heavy word group *locenra bēaga* occupies the overlapping foot. Examples (77a) and (77b) differ only with with respect to non-radical syllables, and therefore have the same hierarchical structure (given above as (69)). Verses with this structure should not appear in the second half-line, and in fact they do not, whether normal or hypermetrical. In abbreviated notation, we will now represent verses like (77b) as Sx//(x)Sxx/Sx. A hypermetrical verse like *mon on middangearde* (37b) will have the representation Sx/Sxsx, since *middangearde* is an ordinary compound formation.

The b-verses characteristic of hypermetrical clusters also have analogues among normal verses:

(78) (a) on // bearm / scipes 35b
 in the-bosom of-the-ship
 "in the ship's hold"

    (b) þǣr þā // gōdan / twēgen 1163b
 where the good two
 "where the two noble ones"

In shorthand notation, we can represent (78a) as x//S/Sx and (78b) as xx//Sx/Sx. The two verses differ only with respect to non-radical syllables, and (47) applies to both in the same way. The hierar-

chical structure of (78b), represented below, will therefore correspond to (78a) as well:

(79)

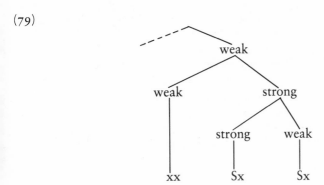

Here (47) has applied within the overlapping foot, marking its
first constituent strong and creating a higher-level strong node.
Since only one S position is marked for alliteration, (78b) may
appear in the second half-line.

Hypermetrical patterns seem to have undergone a considerable
degree of standardization. Most hypermetrical a-verses have the
structure represented in (69), like (77b). Most hypermetrical b-
verses have the structure represented in (79), like (78b). Such standardization would have helped to mitigate the innate complexity
of hypermetrical verses, but the lack of variety makes it difficult to
find evidence for claims about underlying structure. Fortunately,
Genesis A happens to contain what looks like the crucial case:

(80) egesa // (on) brēostum / wunode 2867a
      awe in breast dwelt
      "awe was in (his) heart"
      [Sx//(x)Sxsx]

Genesis A is comparable to *Beowulf* in style and perhaps also in
date (see ASPR, vol. 1, xxvi-xxvii). Some problems arise in the
peculiar line 2869, a locus of editorial emendation, but the remaining 62 hypermetrical verses correspond well to those of *Beowulf,* and obey the constraints on alliteration proposed here.
Example (80) is one of three hypermetrical a-verses in *Genesis A*

with a finite verb at the end of the overlapping foot, and it is the sole hypermetrical a-verse in the poem that lacks double alliteration (only the root syllable of *egesa* alliterates). Such a verse would have the hierarchical structure of (54), which requires only one alliterating syllable (cf. (64a-b)).

The poetic corpus does contain some hypermetrical verses that violate the rules observed in the longer narrative poems. However, the exceptions, which tend to appear in certain works, are for the most part regarded as anomalous by editors. *Maxims I* and *Maxims II* include the lion's share of deviant hypermetrical patterns. These collections of miscellaneous proverbs may represent a distinct poetic tradition if they are not simply corrupt (see Bliss 1958, sections 109–11).

8.8 Hypermetrical Verses and Normal Verses

Like Sievers, we now analyze many hypermetrical verses as foot pairs preceded by an additional foot. Within our theory, many normal patterns also contain embedded foot pairs. Rule II never tolerates an unsubordinated third foot, however. In any verse with three S positions, whether normal or hypermetrical, rule (47) must apply to create a higher-level foot.

At this point the notion of combining smaller feet to form larger feet may begin to seem somewhat less peculiar. If hypermetrical patterns had three feet, they would differ in that respect from the vast majority of other verses, and it would be difficult to understand why they occurred at all. If hypermetrical patterns have a binary structure, on the other hand, we confront the fact that their second foot corresponds to two normal feet. The concept of a higher-level foot is already implicit in hypermetrical patterns. By extending this concept to analysis of the heavier normal patterns, we obtain a simpler rule system that explains the placement of alliterating syllables in all types of verses.

9

WORDS OF CLASSES B AND C

9.1 Emphatic Verbs and Unemphatic Verbs

Campbell (OEG, section 93) states that Old English finite verbs appearing late in the clause had a significant degree of stress but were less prominent than nouns or adjectives. As we have seen in section 8.2, such *emphatic verbs* could mimic the secondary constituents of compounds, and may have undergone a similar degree of subordination.[1] When finite verbs appeared earlier in the clause, their relative prominence was further reduced. The evidence cited by Kuhn (1933, sections 17–20) indicates that such *unemphatic verbs* had a prominence less than that of emphatic verbs but greater than that of auxiliaries or other function words with zero stress. It seems reasonable to suppose that unemphatic verbs bore a reduced stress analogous to the stress on the subordinated root syllable of a lexicalized form such as *Bēowulfes*. The meter shows that syllables with reduced stress differed from those with secondary or zero stress, but the difference may not have been acoustic. Possibly the finer distinctions of relative prominence existed only at the more abstract level where phonological rules apply (cf. Hayes 1983, 391).

9.2 Metrical Interpretation of Weakly Stressed Syllables

Rules (4b-c) distinguish sharply between syllables with secondary stress, which never correspond to metrical x, and syllables with zero stress, which always correspond to metrical x. Syllables with reduced stress evade the labeling restrictions, however, and may occupy any type of metrical position. Verses (17a-b) show that the

secondary constituent *-wulf* in *Bēowulf* can occupy an x position
or an s position. There are also clear cases in which a syllable with
reduced stress occupies an S position:

(81) (a)   Eormen- / rīces 1201a
           Great- King's
           "of Ermanaric"
           [Sx/Sx]

     (b)   ellen- / līce 2122a
           bold-fashion
           "boldly"
           [Sx/Sx]

Bauer (1983, section 3.2.2) states that many institutionalized
forms undergoing the process of lexicalization are "transparent,"
in the sense that speakers remain aware of their constituent
structure. The reduced stress in the secondary constituents of
words like *Eormenrīces* and *ellenlīce* indicates a certain degree of
lexicalization (cf. OEG, section 88). Nevertheless, rule (3a) accepts the internal boundaries of these forms as equivalent to the
internal boundaries of compounds. Evidently Old English speakers remained aware that *-rīc* and *-līce* were related to independent forms such as *rīce* "powerful, powerful man" and *līc* "body,
form, fashion."

The framework employed here makes it possible to explain several metrical peculiarities of unemphatic verbs, some well known,
others less so. With respect to alliteration, the root syllables in
these verbs have exactly the properties that our theory assigns to
syllables of reduced stress, differing from syllables of zero stress
on the one hand and from syllables of secondary stress on the
other.

9.3 Alliteration and Function Words

Alliteration is characteristic of stressed syllables, and no alliterating syllable can correspond to metrical x (cf. (50c)). As the following verses make clear, any similarity between the first constituent
of an unstressed syllable and the first constituent of a stressed
syllable is dismissed as insignificant:

(82) (a) Swylce hē / siomian geseah 2767a
likewise he hang saw
"he also saw hanging"
[(xx)x/Sxxs, not Sx/(x)Sxxs]

(b) hēo under / heolfre genam 1302b
she under gore took
"gory as it was, she took (it)"
[x(xx)/Sxxs, not S/(xx)Sxxs]

If the conjunction *Swylce* corresponded to metrical Sx in (82a), the verse would have the pattern Sx/(x)Sxxs, with the hierarchical structure of (54). This structure does not allow for an alliterating syllable on the s of the second foot. Hence the alliteration on -*seah* would render (82a) unmetrical. If *Swylce* corresponds to the sequence xx, however, the verse analyzes as (xx)x/Sxxs, a variant of type B. In this pattern, the second foot does not undergo subordination to the first, and the s position may contain an alliterating syllable (cf. (51)). Despite its initial *S-*, unstressed *Swylce* does not participate in the alliteration with *seomian* and -*seah*. Similar reasoning applies to (82b). If the pronoun *hēo* occupied an S position in (82b), the alliteration on *heolfre* would render this b-verse unmetrical. Clearly, *hēo* corresponds to metrical x rather than to metrical S, and does not alliterate significantly with *heolfre*.

9.4 Metrical Differences between Unemphatic Verbs and Function Words

Alliteration on a syllable with reduced stress must always be regarded as significant. When a finite verb stands at the beginning of the verse, its root syllable may occupy an S position:

(83) (a) worhte // wǣpna / smið 1452a
worked of-weapons smith
"the weaponsmith made (it)"
[Sx//Sx/S, not xx//Sx/s]

(b) *hēold // heofena / helm
ruled of-heavens guardian
"the guardian of heaven held sway"
[S//Sx/S]

If alliterating verbs like *worhte* corresponded to metrical xx, (83a) would have the pattern xx//Sx/S. Its hierarchical structure would be like (79) except that the highest-level node (representing the a-verse) would be strong rather than weak. Since the second S in such a pattern is dominated by only one weak node, it may contain a second alliterating syllable.[2] Yet we find no verses like (83b), and verses like (83a) occur only in the first half-line. These facts fall into place if we take (83a) as an instance of the pattern Sx//Sx/S. In such a pattern, alliteration is obligatory on the first and second S positions but forbidden on the third S position (cf. (69)). Hence the absence of verses like (83b).[3]

When an unemphatic verb occupies the first foot without alliterating, the second foot shows no evidence of subordination, and may contain two alliterating syllables:

(84)   gebād // wintra / worn 264a
       endured of-winters many
       "endured for many years"
       [xx//Sx/S, not (x)S//Sx/S]

Although the root syllable of *worhte* must occupy an S position in (83a), the root syllable of *gebād* in (84) cannot occupy an S position. If (84) had the pattern (x)S//Sx/S, with the hierarchical structure of (69), its final S would be dominated by two weak nodes, and the alliteration on *worn* would violate (50b). In the pattern (x)S//Sx/S, moreover, rule (47) will assign metrical stress to the first S of the verse, which must therefore contain an alliterating syllable. When occupying the first foot of such a pattern, *gebād* could not fail to alliterate as it does in (84). On the other hand, if *gebād* corresponds to metrical xx, the resulting verse pattern is xx//Sx/S. As we observed just above in connection with (83a), this pattern allows for double alliteration in the second (higher-level) foot.

We conclude that the root syllable in an unemphatic verb corresponds to metrical S in some verses and to metrical x in others. That is exactly what we would expect if such syllables bore reduced stress and could occupy any type of metrical position. When a syllable with reduced stress occupies an S node in the first foot, it alliterates obligatorily, and the following foot is subordinated. Occupying an x position, a syllable with reduced stress cannot alliterate, and the following foot will remain unsubordinated. From this point of view it would be somewhat imprecise to say that unemphatic verbs alliterate optionally. The option is provided by the matching rules, which allow for varying metrical interpretation of syllables with reduced stress. The alliterative rules governing abstract metrical patterns apply without exception.

9.5 Interpretation of Trisyllabic Verb Forms

Our theory also explains a peculiar characteristic of unemphatic verbs with three syllables. Consider the following:

(85) (a) Gespræc / (þā se) gōda 675a   (alliteration on g-)
         spoke then the good-one
         "the noble man spoke"
         [xx/(xx)Sx]

     (b) *tryddode / (se) gōda   (alliteration on g-)
         advanced the good-one
         "the noble man advanced"
         [xxx/(x)Sx]

     (c) tryddode / tīr-fæst 922a
         advanced glory-fast
         "the glorious one advanced"
         [Sxx/Ss]

     (d) forlēton // eorla / gestrēon 3166a   (alliteration on eo-)
         allowed . . . the treasure of earls
         "they allowed . . . the treasure of earls"
         (rest of clause delayed)
         [(x)xx//Sxx/S]

Verses like (85a) are common, but none like (85b) occur. A trisyllabic verb occupying the first foot always alliterates, as in (85c). Now the examples in (83) show that finite verbs have a significant stress, unlike the function words of (82), which have zero stress. Moreover, as we noted in section 1.4, Old English has no unstressed words with three syllables. Verbs like *worhte* can mimic the behavior of nouns like *dryhten* or of conjunctions like *oþþe*, but no such option exists for *tryddode,* which always corresponds to Sxx (cf. section 5.2). When *tryddode* stands first in the verse, its root syllable always corresponds to the first S, which is designated for alliteration by (47) and (68b). Note that the form *forlēton* in (85d) cannot be regarded as trisyllabic. Its "unstressed prefix" *for-* counts as a separate word.

9.6 Interpretation of Verse-medial Finite Verbs

The word order of the verse in *Beowulf* is to a large extent that of the early Germanic period, when the verb stood at the beginning or end of the clause (Klaeber 1950, xciv). No verse in the poem has subject-verb-object word order when subject, verb, and object are words of major category. The metrical value of a finite verb in medial position is therefore somewhat difficult to determine. Some relevant evidence does exist, however. The first two verses below are from *Beowulf;* the third is supplied from *Widsith:*

(86) (a)   God wāt on / mec 2650b
           God knows on me
           "As for me, God knows"
           [Ssx/S]

     (b)   (æt) fōtum // (sæt) frēan / Scyldinga 1166a
           at feet sat of-the-lord of-the Scyldings
           "sat at the feet of the lord of the Scyldings"
           [(x)Sx//(x)S/Sxx]

     (c)   Offa / (wēold) Ongle 35a
           Offa ruled Anglen
           "Offa ruled Anglen"
           [Sx/(x)Sx]

In (86a), assignment of *wāt* to an x position would yield the unmetrical verse pattern Sxx/S, which would overlap the foot pattern Sxxs (cf. section 2.3). Assignment of *wāt* to an s position yields the acceptable type E pattern Ssx/S. The Ssx/S analysis presupposes that the adverbial phrase *on mec* modifies the whole clause *God wāt* rather than the verb. If *on mec* modifies the verb *wāt,* the major constituent break would fall after *God,* and the verse would analyze as S/Sxs. Under either interpretation of the syntax, assignment of *wāt* to an x position is ruled out. In the hypermetrical (86b), the finite verb *sæt* appears in verse-medial position. Unlike *wāt* in (86a), *sæt* must be assigned to an x position. If *sæt* occupied an s position in (86b), the verse would violate (15a), which rules out patterns of the form Sxs or Sxxs in the first foot of any half-line, whether normal or hypermetrical. The same reasoning applies to (86c), where the finite verb *wēold* functions as an extrametrical word in a normal verse pattern. Note that the alliteration on the root syllable of *Ongle* precludes assignment of *wēold* to the second foot in (86c).

The variant metrical interpretations of *wāt, sæt,* and *wēold* suggest that such forms bore reduced stress, like finite verbs placed at the beginning of the verse. One would not want to overestimate the strength of the evidence in (86a-c), but it does seem to support Campbell's view of clause-medial finite verbs (OEG, section 93).

9.7 Interpretation of Nonclitic Function Words

The stress acquired by nonclitic function words can sometimes be detected by its interaction with the rule of resolution:

(87)   un-sōfte / þonan 2140b   (alliteration on u-)
       not-easily thence
       "with difficulty from that place"
       [Ssx/S, not Ssx/Sx]

When an Ssx compound occupies the first foot, the second foot always contains a monosyllable or resolvable disyllable. If *þonan* stood unresolved, (87) would have a long reversed pattern of the sort ruled out by (15b). In (87), therefore, *þonan* must be resolvable, which means that it must bear some degree of stress (cf. section 1.3).

Nonclitic function words in verse-medial position have received little attention, but it seems that here too they bore some degree of stress. Consider the following:

(88)   Wā bið þǣm / (ðe) sceal 183b
       Woe shall-be to-whom that must
       "It will be woeful for one who must"
       [Ssx/(x)S, not Sxx/(x)S]

Verse (88) contains two nonclitic function words. At the end of the verse, the auxiliary verb *sceal* acquires stress and occupies an S position.[4] The verse-medial copula *bið*, which would normally precede *Wā*, is removed from proclitic position and occupies an s position. The result is a common variant of the type E pattern with an extrametrical word before the second foot (cf. (23)). If *bið* corresponded to metrical x, the verse would analyze as the unmetrical pattern Sxx/(x)S (cf. (86a)). Note that *bið* cannot be proclitic to *þǣm:* if *þǣm* had clause-final stress here, the unmetrical pattern Sxs/(x)S would be produced. Evidently *þǣm* was regarded as a relative pronoun belonging to the subordinate clause, and *bið* was clause-final. Examples like (88) are rare because clause boundaries do not ordinarily occur in verse-medial position. This unusual instance of the type E pattern can encompass a relatively large syntactic domain because it consists entirely of monosyllabic words.

9.8 Interpretation of Adverbs

Campbell (OEG, section 94) divides adverbs into two groups with differing relative prominence. The first group includes sentential adverbs like *oft* "often" and vague intensifiers like *micle* "much." When adverbs of this type occupy the first foot, their root syllables may correspond to metrical S or to metrical x, like the root syllables of finite verbs:

(89) (a) þæt mē is micle / lēofre 2651a   (alliteration on l-)
          that to-me is much preferable
          "I would much rather"
          [(xxx)xx/Sx]

     (b) Oft // Scyld / Scēfing 4a
          Often Scyld Scefing
          "Often Scyld Scefing . . . "
          [x//S/Sx]

     (c) oft be- / witigað 1428b   (alliteration on o-)
          often observe
          "often observe"
          [Sx/Sx]

In (89a), *micle* corresponds to metrical xx, and does not alliterate (cf. (85a)). In (89b), *Oft* corresponds to metrical x, and the following foot remains unsubordinated, as the double alliteration shows (cf. (84)). In (89c), *oft* occupies an S position in the first foot of a b-verse and takes the alliteration.

The metrical interpretation of sentential adverbs and intensifiers varies in verse-medial position. Consider the following:

(90) (a) Hafa nū ond / (ge-)heald 658a
           have now and hold
           "preserve and keep safe now"
           [Ssx/(x)S]

     (b) Heald þū / (nū), hrūse 2247a
           hold thou now, earth
           "hold now, earth"
           [Sx/(x)Sx]

In (90a), assignment of *nū* to an x position would result in an unattested pattern Sxx/(xx)S (cf. section 2.3). Evidently *nū* occupies an s position in a type E pattern Ssx/(x)S, with an extrametrical syllable before the second foot (cf. (23), (88)). In (90b), *nū* must correspond to metrical x. Otherwise, (90b) would have a long reversed pattern Sxs/Sx with the complex foot Sxs in first position (cf. (86b)).[5]

Campbell's second group consists of "defining" adverbs that restrict the meaning of a following verb or adjective. These behave like class A words, and their root syllables do not occupy x positions:

(91) (a) wīde / (ge-) sȳne 1403b   (alliteration on w-)
           widely seen
           "widely seen"
           [Sx/(x)Sx]

     (b) Fyrst / forð gewāt 210a
           time forth went
           "time passed on"
           [S/Sxs]

     (c) weras / on sāwon 1650b   (alliteration on w-)
           men on looked
           "men looked on"
           [S/Ssx]

(d) Hygd / swīðe geong 1926b[6]
  Hygd extremely young
  "Hygd (was) extremely young"
  [S/Sxs]

In (91a), the root syllable of the defining adverb *wīde* occupies the
first S position in a type A1 pattern, and alliterates obligatorily.
There are no verses in which a defining adverb occupies x positions of the first foot while the following constituent alliterates. In
(91b-d), the major constituent break falls after the first word, and
word groups with defining adverbs occupy the second foot.
Campbell (OEG, section 94 note 1) states that adverbs like *forð,
on,* and *swīðe* can subordinate a following verb or adjective to
form a quasi-compound. Accordingly, I have assigned the root
syllables of *gewāt, sāwon,* and *geong* to s positions in patterns
with the hierarchical structure of (54). This structure allows for a
second alliterating syllable on the S of the second foot (as in
(91b)), but also permits single alliteration (as in (91c-d)). The
single alliteration in (91c) comes as no surprise, since the root
syllable of clause-final verbs like *sāwon* may occupy an s position
in any case (cf. (64a-b)). The single alliteration in (91d) is of
special interest, however. Adjectives like *geong* usually occupy S
positions, and verses quite similar to (91d) have obligatory alliteration in the second foot (cf. (63a-d)). Example (91d) and the
two other verses like it provide good evidence for Campbell's
claim that a defining adverb subordinated a following adjective. It
is important to note that *swīðe* functions as a defining adverb in
(91d), not as a vague intensifier. In (89a), *micle* simply adds emphasis to a declaration by the loyal retainer Wiglaf, who would
"much rather" die than abandon his lord. In (91d), the poet
wishes to point out that Hygd was a child bride. In that context,
"young" and "very young" mean quite different things.

9.9 Subordination of Class A Words

Words of class A do not usually undergo subordination to other
words within the restricted confines of the half-line. Hence we can
usually speak as if their root syllables had primary stress. In cases
like (91d), however, our analysis must take into account the syntactic relation of the class A word to other words sharing the same

verse. Cases like the following also require a more sophisticated analysis:

(92) (a) (Ic) ðæt / mǣl geman 2633a   (alliteration on m-)
I that time remember
"I remember that time"
[(x)x/Sxs]

   (b) Mǣl is / (mē tō) fēran 316a   (alliteration on f-)
Time is for-me to go
"It is time for me to go"
[xx/(xx)Sx]

   (c) sēcean / wolde 200b   (alliteration on s-)
seek would
"intended to seek"
[Sx/Sx]

   (d) sēcean // wynlēas / wīc 821a   (alliteration on w-)
to-seek joyless dwelling
"to seek out a gloomy home"
[xx//Sx/S]

In (92a), the noun *mǣl* "time" has the greatest relative prominence in its clause, and occupies an S position. In syntactic structures like that of (92b), however, the predicate noun has reduced stress, and occupies an x position. The Eddic poetry of Scandinavia contains some striking parallels to (92b), including the practically identical half-line *Mál er mér at ríða* "It is time for me to ride," alliterating on *r-* (Neckel and Kuhn 1962, 160). Kuhn (1933, section 27) provides several additional examples. When an infinitive verb occupies the first foot, the second foot usually contains a weakly stressed auxiliary verb. In such cases, exemplified by (92c), the root syllable of the infinitive always occupies an S position, and alliterates obligatorily, like the root syllable of a verse-initial noun or adjective. Occasionally a clause-initial infinitive shares the verse with a noun phrase. In cases like (92d), apparently, the noun phrase subordinates the infinitive, and the root syllable of the infinitive can occupy an x position, like the root syllable of a finite verb. If the infinitive in (92d) corresponded to metrical Sx rather than to metrical xx, the verse would have the hierarchical structure of (69), and its alliterative pattern would be unacceptable (cf. (84)).

9.10 Enclitics

Conjunctions and other clitics never have metrical prominence. Their root syllables always occupy x positions, and never alliterate significantly. True "prepositions" – those preposed to the governed constituent – behave like clitics, except when the governed constituent is itself enclitic to the preposition. In that case, the preposition can acquire clause-final stress, and may alliterate. Sievers (1893, section 28) provides the following example from the *Phoenix:*

(93) and / æfter þon 238b
      and after that
      "and afterwards"
      [x/Sxx]

Here clause-final stress falls on *æfter* rather than on the enclitic *þon.* Hence *æfter* alliterates and *þon* occupies an x position.[7] Example (93) is of some interest because enclitics do not occur very frequently in Old English (see OEG, sections 83–6). Word groups occupying the pattern Sxx normally appear verse-initially, with a proclitic as the final constituent of the foot (cf. (9c)). The example above is one of very few in which a verse-final foot of the form Sxx contains a word group.

9.11 Contrastive Stress and Emphatic Stress

The root syllable of a function word placed near the beginning of the sentence normally occupies an x position. In a few cases, however, a pronoun or demonstrative that would normally be unstressed seems to acquire a contrastive stress that allows it to occupy an S position. Consider the following example, with alliteration on *þā-:*

(94) þon / þā dydon 44b
      than those did
      "than *those* did"
      [x/Ssx]

Here it seems reasonable to posit a contrastive stress on þā distinguishing the people who did the action being discussed from the people mentioned earlier in 43a as hī "they" (cf. OEG, section 99). It is important to note the difference between contrastive stress, which occurs under specific grammatical conditions, and the sort of "emphatic stress" that may occur optionally on any constituent. Emphatic stress is optional in sentences like "These cigarettes taste great, *and* they are mild." In sentences like "They were no less generous than *those* men," on the other hand, the contrastive stress is obligatory. Rules of contrastive stress are comparable to other phrasal stress rules, and our theory may properly regard them as significant (cf. Hayes 1983, 383). Hence (94) need not be regarded as an exception to the labeling rule (2b), which restricts all syllables with zero stress to x positions. It is important to note that the *Beowulf* poet never alliterates on conjunctions, not even when they could bear the sort of emphasis illustrated in the Modern English example above.

Although the metrical rules take no account of emphatic stress, the poet might select one metrical option rather than another for purposes of rhetorical emphasis (cf. OEG, 99). In assigning syllables with reduced stress to S positions, for example, the *Beowulf* poet may have taken into account the narrative value of the word in question. The metrical prominence that coincides with alliteration could enhance the storytelling value of a vivid finite verb in unemphatic position.[8] If the unemphatic verb had a primarily syntactic function, on the other hand, assignment of its root syllable to metrical x could indicate its subordinate narrative status, and the metrical prominence could fall on a more vivid word in the second foot. A similar type of stylistic preference has often been observed in English rhymed verse. The best poets in this tradition prefer rhetorically prominent words for rhymes even though the metrical rules allow for free employment of meaningless "tags."

9.12 Linguistic Prominence and Double Alliteration

When an alliterating word of class B occupies the first foot, a word of class A in the second foot usually alliterates as well. Consider the following:

(95) (a)   (Ge-)munde / (þā se) gōda 758a   (alliteration on m-)
           remembered then the good-one
           "then the noble man remembered"
           [(x)Sx/(xx)Sx]

     (b)   (ne ge-)feah hē / (þǣre) fǣhðe 109a
           not rejoiced he of-that feud
           "he got no pleasure from that feud"
           [(xx)Sx/(xx)Sx]

     (c)   Gespræc / (þā se) gōda 675a   (alliteration on g-)
           spoke then the good-one
           "then the noble man spoke"
           [xx/(xx)Sx]

Verses like (95a), in which the finite verb alliterates but the following noun does not, are quite rare. If such verses occurred much less frequently, we might be tempted to dismiss them as unmetrical (but cf. 1537a, 1548b, 2980b). Much more common are verses like (95b-c), in which the noun occupying the second foot alliterates (cf. Klaeber 1950, 280, 4a). It seems that the most prominent linguistic stress in the verse normally participates in the alliteration even when it occupies a relatively weak metrical position.

9.13 Linguistic Stress and Metrical Stress

The theory of metrical stress proposed here explains the attested alliterative patterns in a coherent way and has some value as a tool for investigating relative prominence relations within the confines of the verse. If we factor out the effects of (47), it becomes possible to formulate rules of phrasal stress that operate consistently in all verses with the same grammatical pattern. The results will not seem very surprising to those familiar with previous work on Old English meter, which has generally assumed an indirect relation between alliteration and linguistic stress (cf. Sievers 1893, sections 18–29). If we claimed that alliterative patterns expressed relative linguistic prominence directly, we would have to argue that a-verses with double alliteration had a stress contour differing from that of b-verses with the same syntax. No one, to my knowledge, has offered such an argument. The problem has been to distinguish linguistic factors affecting the probability of alliteration from the metrical factors that also play a significant role.

Although we have used the concept of metrical subordination primarily to explain alliterative patterns, this feature of the theory also helps to explain a peculiarity of resolution. All short syllables with primary stress normally undergo resolution. However, such syllables often stand unresolved towards the end of the verse: rule (27c) makes resolution obligatory only for the first S. Such a rule would appear to conflict with the general principle that correspondence to metrical patterns tends to be lax at the beginnings of units and strict at the ends (Hayes 1983, 373; cf. (29)). The paradox resolves itself when we consider that the probability of resolution is only partly dependent on linguistic stress. Resolution occurs more often on S positions than on s positions independently of the type of syllable that happens to occupy those positions (cf. (27b), (28a-f) and accompanying discussion). In general, then, we would expect a correlation between resolution and metrical strength. As it turns out, the positions of obligatory resolution are the strongest metrical positions in the line, as defined by (47). If resolution is obligatory for a metrical position, that position must also contain an alliterating syllable. Both alliteration and resolution are intimately related to linguistic stress, but both are also affected by a rule of metrical stress peculiar to the poetry.

10

RULES AND EXCEPTIONS

10.1 The Status of Exceptions in a Systematic Theory

We noted above (section 2.6) that the lack of generalized metrical constraints in Sievers's theory makes it difficult to distinguish unusual verses from genuine exceptions. Editors often emend verses with a pattern attested only once or twice, but since Sievers allows for subtypes with very few members there is no well-defined boundary between unmetrical patterns and the more complex variants of "basic" patterns. Within the theory proposed here, the definition of "unmetrical" is independent of statistical frequency. A complex verse is one that deviates considerably from the norm without violating a categorical rule. Any verse that violates a categorical rule is unmetrical.

10.2 Apparent Exceptions

Bliss (1958, sections 84–7) argues for the existence of a few patterns that our theory cannot accommodate. As it turns out, most of the verses offered by Bliss as evidence have alternative interpretations acceptable to the theory. Let us first consider the evidence for a pattern Sxx/S, which we have ruled out by the overlap constraint (12):

(96) (a)   ēam his nefan 881a
           the-uncle to-his nephew
           "the uncle to his nephew"

(b) dǣdum gefremed 954a
     by-deeds accomplished
     "accomplished by your acts"

(c) Raþe æfter þon 724b
     Quickly after that
     "Immediately afterwards"

(d) rǣhte ongēan 747b
     reached against
     "reached out at"

(e) lissa gelong 2150a
     of-joys dependent
     "joys dependent (on you)"

Our version of the resolution rule allows for analysis of (96a-b) as instances of the pattern Sx/(x)Sx with an unresolved syllable in the second foot (cf. (28e)). These, then, cause no problems. Bliss's analysis of (96c) overlooks the evidence supplied by Sievers (1893, section 28) showing that þon is enclitic to æfter in the expression æfter þon "after that" (see (93) and accompanying discussion). If we interpret þon as an enclitic, the verse qualifies as an instance of the acceptable pattern S/Sxx. Example (96d) would be difficult to explain if it were not suspect on paleographical grounds. This string of words is immediately preceded in the manuscript by an unusual smudged blank space that probably represents "an erasure of some five letters" (Zupitza-Davis, 36). We must therefore reckon with the possibility that a scribe or corrector erased the first foot of an x/Sxxs or S/Sxxs pattern without replacing it (see Dobbie 1953, 153).

We are left with (96e), a notorious metrical crux. Dobbie (1953, 227) cites as supporting evidence for this pattern *Guthlac* 312b-13a, *Nis mē wiht æt ēow / lēofes gelong* "Nothing you have seems desirable to me." The parallel between *Beowulf* 2150a and *Guthlac* 313a is admittedly intriguing, though the extreme rarity of the Sxx/S pattern remains unexplained. Several emendations have of course been proposed, but none has achieved consensus (see Pope 1942, 321). As it turns out, we can interpret the manuscript in such a way as to obtain an acceptable verse. I would represent 2149b-50a as *Gēn is eall æt ðē* / *liss ā gelong* "Still, as always, joy is dependent on you." *Gēn* "still" and *ā* "always" frequently appear in the same clause, despite what may seem a partial redundancy of meaning. When adjacent, the two forms are spelled as a single word, *gena,* printed as *gēna* by editors who indicate vowel length.[1] The relations of constituency in 2149b-50a are somewhat complex, as in most phrases with adverbials. It seems likely, however, that *Gēn* and *ā* both function as sentential adverbs. On that hypothesis, *ā* would be in close constituency with the verb *is* in the preceding verse. The major constituent break in 2150a would fall between *ā* and *gelong,* and the verse would analyze as the type E pattern Ssx/S, with the sentential adverb occupying an s position (cf. (90a)). The word order of 2149b-50a might have seemed slightly unusual: sentential adverbs normally stand together at the beginning of the clause. However, poets clearly do split adverb pairs for metrical reasons. In *Christ* 299b-300b, for example, we find the clause *ond þē, Maria, forð* / *efne unwemme* / *ā gehealdan* "and, Mary, to keep yourself henceforth ever entirely unblemished." Normally *ā* and *forð* would stand together.[2] In the *Christ* passage, the poet delays *ā* to provide an alliterating syllable for 300b.

Those who believe that *Guthlac* 313a validates the reading *lissa gelong* should consider the following line from the *Paris Psalter* (61.1), a striking parallel with our revised interpretation:

(97)   æt him is hǣlu mīn hēr eall gelancg
       at him is prosperity mine here all dependent
       "all my prosperity in this world is dependent on Him"

In *Beowulf,* King Hrothgar says that present joy is due to the power of the hero. In the *Paris Psalter,* we see an apparent displacement of this epic concept to the religious sphere, with God as the all-powerful savior. Here *eall* is in close constituency with *hǣlu* of the preceding verse, and the major constituent break comes before *gelancg,* a variant spelling of *gelong.* As in our new reading of 2150a, *liss ā gelong,* the weakly stressed particle occupies the s position of the pattern Ssx/S.

It should be emphasized that *liss ā gelong* does not constitute an emendation, but a reinterpretation of manuscript evidence. The absence of conspicuous word spaces on both sides of the letter *a* does not prove that the scribe regarded it as part of an adjacent word. The particle *ā* is often run together with an adjacent word, usually with the word to the right (as in 283a, 455b, 779a, 881b, 930b, 1478b). The attachment of *ā* to *liss* in 2150a may indicate the close syntactic and metrical relation linking *ā* with preceding material. It is worth noting that even unstressed prefixes are sometimes attached to the preceding constituent rather than to the following constituent (see Dobbie 1953, xviii-xix).

Verse patterns of the form S/Sx and Sx/S would overlap the foot patterns Ssx and Sxs, respectively, and would also violate the verse length rule (13a). Bliss cites four verses as evidence for such patterns:

(98) (a)   bord wið rond 2673a
           shield with border
           "the shield together with its reinforcing rim"

     (b)   secg betsta 947a, 1759a
           warrior best
           "best warrior"

     (c)   ðegn betstan 1871b
           thane best
           "best thane"

Pope (1942, 320) dispensed with (98a) by showing that it results from a misreading of the manuscript. What Klaeber prints as *Līgȳðum forborn bord wið rond* should in fact read *Līg ȳðum fōr; born bord wið rond* "The fire moved forward in surges; the shield burned together with its supporting rim." The proper reading of 2673a, *born bord wið rond*, qualifies as an instance of the S//Sx/S pattern (type Db). Pope's interpretation is now standard (cf. Dobbie 1953; Wrenn and Bolton 1973).

The spellings *betsta, betstan* in (98b-c) correspond to bisyllabic forms resulting from a rule of syncopation that operated in some Old English dialects (see Amos 1980, 18–29). If syncopated forms must be posited in (98b-c), the verses have only enough linguistic material to occupy three metrical positions. Pope (1942, 320) suggested that we should posit *secg betesta, ðegn betestan*, without syncopation. On this hypothesis, (98b-c) qualify as instances of the type Da pattern S/Sxx. However, the verses are still regarded as problematic because of evidence offered by Sievers (1885, 462–3) suggesting that the poet's dialect had syncopated forms only.

It seems to me that Sievers's view of syncopation can be reconciled with Pope's reading of (98b-c). The key is a peculiarity of the phonological sequence *st,* which is associated with certain irregularities of Old English syllabification (for theoretical discussion of related problems see Lowenstamm 1981). The sequence *st* occurs word-initially in Old English, and might therefore occur as syllabic onset in medial position. If it did act as syllabic onset, *st* would leave the preceding syllable open; otherwise, the *s* of *st* would close the preceding syllable. Because syncopation occurs in open syllables only, variation with respect to syncopation before *st* would not be surprising. Spelling evidence shows that such variation did in fact occur (see OEG, sections 352, 388–9). A regular or variant trisyllabic form *betesta* might well have existed in the *Beowulf* poet's dialect even if syncopation was the rule for forms like *betra* "better" (< *betera*).

Bliss also accepts verse patterns of the form Sxxx/S and Sxxxx/S. Because the initial feet in these patterns do not correspond to Old English word patterns, our theory cannot accommodate them. As possible instances of Sxxx/S and Sxxxx/S Bliss cites the verses displayed below and a few others like them:

(99) (a)   Wā bið þǣm ðe sceal 183b[3]
           Woe shall-be to-whom that must
           "It will be woeful for one who must"

     (b)   dēað ungemete nēah 2728b[4]
           death immeasurably close
           "death was immediately at hand"

We have accounted for verses like (99a) already (see (88) and accompanying discussion). These qualify as instances of the type E pattern Ssx/(x)S, with the clause-final copula occupying an s position. All four verses like (99b) have the same syntax, and all contain the dative adverbial *ungemete* "immediately" or the variant genitive adverbial form *unigmetes*. According to Bliss (1958, section 86), *"ungemete(s),* though unusually long, is an adverb of degree, and must be proclitic on the adjective it qualifies." Our linguistic knowledge is in fact less certain than Bliss suggests. As

we noted in discussion of (91d), Campbell regards sentential adverbs and vague intensifiers as proclitics, but states that adverbs of
degree like *swīðe* can provide the first constituent for a quasi-compound. I do not think that Bliss is right to disregard the "unusual
length" of *ungemete(s):* one would expect only simplex adverbs of
high frequency to be degraded to the status of function words. In
modern English, for example, simplex adverbs like *rather* lose
stress quite often, but more complex formations with a lower
frequency do not do so (contrast *that's rather obvious, that's immediately obvious).* It seems to me, moreover, that *ungemete(s)*
has appreciable semantic content. By the time (99b) occurs, the
poet has already told us several times that Beowulf would die on
the day he confronted the dragon. Verse (99b) does not simply
indicate that Beowulf's death is rather near: it informs us that the
hero, his dying speeches completed, is now actually breathing his
last. We can therefore regard the word group *ungemete nēah* of
(99b) as comparable to *swīðe geong* of (91d), in which the adverb
subordinates the adjective. Anyone who inspects 1792b, 2420b,
and 2721b will conclude, I think, that *ungemete(s)* has significant
content in these lines as well. The choice of a low-frequency,
morphologically complex adverb would seem in general to indicate considered emphasis on the degree of an action or attribute
rather than vague intensification.

If *ungemete* subordinates *nēah,* we can divide (99b) before
-*mete* to produce an acceptable verse pattern:

(100)   dēað unge- / mete nēah 2728b
        death immeasurably close
        "death was immediately at hand"
        [Sxx/Ss]

Here -*mete* undergoes resolution on the S position of the second
foot while the unstressed proclitics *un-* and -*ge-* occupy x positions
in the first foot. The subordinated *nēah* can occupy an s position
rather than an S position, like *geong* in (91d). The pattern Sxx/Ss
has the hierarchical structure represented in (54), which requires
alliteration only on the S of the first foot.

For the most part, then, the verses cited by Bliss as evidence for
exceptional patterns turn out to have less problematic interpretations. With the number of truly exceptional verses reduced to a

handful, it becomes more plausible to explain them in terms of scribal error.

In section 8.6, we dispensed with one apparent exception to the rule that the second constituent of a compound never alliterates unless the first constituent alliterates also. We now confront another apparent exception of this kind:

(101)   fela-sinnigne secg 1379a[5]
        very-sinful man
        "the very sinful man"

Dobbie (1953) retains MS *fela* in his edition, but Klaeber (1950) emends to *sinnigne secg*. The editors assume that *fela-sinnigne* is (or would be) a compound with primary stress on the first constituent. Now it seems clear that *fela* could form compounds or "quasi-compounds" with following adjectives, but I see no reason to believe that it always did so. The situation is confused because the combinative form of *fela* is not distinguished in spelling from other forms with weak stress or zero stress. In order to interpret *fela* plus adjective constructions, therefore, we must turn to an analogous constituent that forms unambiguous compounds.

Consider *swīð-* / *swīðe*, which, like *fela*, has the meaning "very" when functioning as an adverb. The combinative form *swīð-* appears in unambiguous compounds with an adjective as the second constituent (e.g. *swīð-hwæt* "very keen"). However, the non-combinative form also appears with following adjectives (e.g. in *swīðe geong* "very young"). Verses like (91d) show that *swīðe* could subordinate a following adjective to form a quasi-compound. The fact that *swīðe* usually alliterates in preference to a following adjective might also be taken to indicate a "quasi-compound" status for such constructions.[5] On the other hand, *swīðe* might be expected to appear occasionally as a vague intensifier, in which case it could occupy verse-initial weak positions without alliterating (cf. *micle* in (89a)). This does in fact seem to occur. In the second poetic section of *Solomon and Saturn*, for example, we find *swīðe lēoftæle* "very estimable," with alliteration on *l-* (368a). The same situation arises in the hypermetrical 330b, *ðū eart swīðe bittres cynnes* "you are of a very bitter kindred," alliterating on *b-*. *Solomon and Saturn* adheres closely, in hundreds of crucial cases, to the requirement that the first stressed syllable in the verse, when fully stressed, must alliterate (cf. (47), (50)).[6] I see no reason to doubt its testimony with respect to the issue at hand. If *fela* was like *swīðe,* then, it could occur as the first constituent of a compound, as the first constituent of a quasi-compound, and occasionally as a vague intensifier.

Another instructive analogue to *fela* is the very similar *eal(l)* "all, very." Like *fela, eall* usually alliterates in preference to a following adjective, and editors usually print *eall* plus adjective constructions as compounds (e.g. *eallgylden, Beowulf* 2767b). The usual procedure cannot, however, be followed in *eal langtwīdig, Beowulf* 1708a, alliterating on *l-.* Here we can hardly be dealing with a triple compound *eallangtwīdig.* The embedded double compound in triple compounds is typically a familiar preexisting formation, but *langtwīdig* is a hapax legomenon. In this particular *eall* plus adjective construction, obviously, *eall* is functioning as a weakly stressed adverbial intensifier. Verse (101) is best regarded as evidence that *fela* could be used in the same way.

Further evidence comes from the Old Saxon *Heliand,* verse 4527a (Behaghel-Mitzka, 157):

(102) endi im sagda filu langsamna râd   (allit-
       and him told very long-lasting counsel   eration
       "and gave him eternal counsel"   on l-)

The verse seems very close, both grammatically and metrically, to *fela sinnigne secg* (cf. Behaghel 1897, 36 A.III, where *filu langsamna* is listed as a typical adverb-adjective construction). Old Saxon *suīðo,* the cognate of Old English *swīðe,* can also appear without alliteration before a governed adjective (e.g. in verse 177a, *suuīðo frôd gumo* "a very wise man," alliterating on *f-*).

A verse *fela sinnigne secg* would be perfectly acceptable if *fela* had weak stress or zero stress. The medial syllable in *sinnigne* bears reduced stress, and the word is susceptible of the metrical interpretation Sxx (see OEG, section 89). Hence *fela sinnigne secg* could be analyzed as an instance of the type B pattern $xx//Sxx/S$ (cf. the similar verses (19b) and (92d)).

The two Thorkelin transcripts date from a period when the *Beowulf* manuscript was still fairly well preserved.[7] With their help, one can still determine what the scribe wrote in all but a small percentage of cases.[8] Metrists generally exclude a half-line from consideration when there is serious doubt about how to read the manuscript; but two questionable readings have figured as evidence in relatively recent publications. I will consider these briefly before turning to the genuine exceptions.

In Zupitza-Davis (p. 126), verse 2714b appears as *bealo-nið weoll* (i.e., *bealo-nīð wēoll*), which could mean "deadly malice surged." The first syllable of *bealo-*, which is short, must undergo resolution, creating the unmetrical verse pattern Ss/S. Keyser (1969, 350) objects to "emendation" of this line, but *bealo-nīð wēoll* is nothing more than one possible interpretation of available evidence. In the manuscript, all that can now be read of the first word is *beal-*. Thorkelin A, the work of the unidentified copyist, reads *bealomð;* Thorkelin B, the work of Thorkelin himself, reads *bealo niði*. Most modern editors print *bealo-nīðe wēoll* "surged with deadly malice," an interpretation that accords well with the poet's style. The *Beowulf* poet employs the form *wēol(l)* ten times at the end of the verse, and in seven instances *wēol(l)* is immediately preceded by a dative adverbial noun (cf. 849b, *heoro-drēore wēol* "surged with battle-blood"). According to Dobbie (1953, 244), "in the hand of the second scribe, the heavy vertical stroke of *e* may easily be mistaken for an *i* if the letter is at all obscure." Dobbie concludes that "the reading *-niði* in transcript B undoubtedly reflects a *-niðe* in the MS." Dobbie's note gives several additional examples of *i* in the transcripts for *e* in the manuscript. The usual emendation seems to represent the best way of interpreting available evidence.

In the manuscript, verses 1980b-81b appear as *meodu scencum hwearf · geond þæt side reced hæreðes dohtor,* which might be translated, "Hareth's daughter circulated throughout that large hall with cups of mead." According to Zupitza-Davis (p. 91), *side (sīde),* which appears above the line, represents an addition in different ink but probably in the same hand. Most editors print 1980b as *Meoduscencum hwearf.* This leaves line 1981 without alliteration. Some scholars willing to tolerate odd patterns advocate including *hwearf* in 1981a to supply alliteration with *hæreðes* (see Keyser 1969, 349–50; Wrenn and Bolton 1973, 170). However, this interpretation of the text presupposes a number of peculiarities in a very small space. With *hwearf* removed from 1980b, the resulting verse, *Meoduscencum,* fills only three metrical positions (note that the first syllable of *Meodu-* is short, and must undergo resolution by (27c)). Moving *hwearf* into 1981a does very little to improve matters there. A verse *hwearf geond þæt sīde reced* would have the complex pattern Sxx//S/S, with a heavy word group in the second foot. This pattern has the hierarchical structure represented in (69), for which double alliteration is obligatory. If we throw out the supralinear *sīde,* the resulting *hwearf geond þæt reced* would barely attain to metricality, if at all. Like the unusual (95a), such a verse would have alliteration on the finite verb without alliteration on the accompanying noun. Moreover, the short, fully stressed syllable of *reced* would stand unresolved on an S position, as in the rare type represented by (28e). Manuscript punctuation poses another problem. According to Dobbie (1953, xxx), the type of small raised dot that follows *hwearf* appears somewhat less than seven hundred times in the *Beowulf* manuscript. Such "pointing" indicates the end of the half-line in all but thirteen cases. Inclusion of *hwearf* in 1981a seems, then, to create a great many problems and to solve very few. As evidence for rare metrical patterns, this vexed stretch of manuscript has little value.

10.3 Unmetrical Verses in the Manuscript

The text of *Beowulf* contains a number of clearly unmetrical verses. Twenty-one lines have metrical defects coinciding with defects of sense or grammar.[9] In eight of these, alliteration fails to occur. Alliteration is also missing in seven other lines,[10] and there are two instances of double alliteration in the b-verse.[11] Such anomalies must obviously be excluded from the corpus chosen as the basis for a metrical theory. Those that make sense are so irregular that even conservative editors regard them as errors. The remainder have defects independent of the meter, and cannot provide reliable evidence for or against a given theory.

Our theory also isolates a few unmetrical half-lines with somewhat less obvious defects. These constitute a subset of the verses rejected by Sievers, and are regarded as peculiar by all modern editors. A theory that failed to isolate a few such unmetrical verses would be implausible because it would imply an accuracy of scribal transmission nowhere in evidence. Verse passages surviving in more than one manuscript show that scribal errors yielding a satisfactory meaning occurred with significant frequency. A number of these errors produced unmetrical verses (see Sisam 1953, 29–44).

Most of the unmetrical verses can be explained by reference to differences between the poet's idiom and the idiom of the scribe. It is well known that many lexical items employed in poetry were no longer current in ordinary speech (see Klaeber 1950, lxiii). Moreover, the poet's language includes some semantically inessential additions, such as the first constituents of poetic compounds. Articles, demonstratives, and similar function words can be added or omitted for metrical reasons, sometimes against prevailing usage (cf. Mitchell 1968, section 193.2; Klaeber 1950, xcii-iii). We would therefore anticipate a tendency on the part of the scribe, perhaps quite unconscious, to replace poetic idioms with idioms more familiar. The meter might serve to inhibit this tendency, but would not necessarily check it in all cases. Lord (1960, 126–7) shows that the slow pace of writing can interfere with perception of metrical regularity in cultures where oral poetic transmission is the norm.

The semantically redundant combinative in a poetic compound is especially vulnerable to scribal misinterpretation or omission. A combinative preserved in the *Junius* manuscript, for example, is missing from the parallel passage in the *Exeter Book:*

(103) (a) sǣ-faroða sand (Daniel 322a)
       sea-beach's sand
       "the sand of the beach"

      (b) swā waroþa sond (Azarias 39a)
       likewise beach's sand
       "and the sand of the beach"

Alliteration in both verses is on *s-. Daniel* 322a is an ordinary type E verse with a poetic compound occupying the first foot. In *Azarias* 39a, the combinative *sǣ-* has been misread as *swā* and the *f-* of *faroða* has been misread as the runic letter "wynn" of the very similar *waroþa. Azarias* 39a makes perfect sense, but it is unmetrical. As a proclitic, *swā* cannot alliterate significantly. Alliteration should fall on the fully stressed radical syllable of *waroþa,* which occupies the first S position.

One or two similar mistakes would be expected in the *Beowulf* manuscript:

(104) (a) in ðām sele Grendeles mōdor 2139
in that hall Grendel's mother
"Grendel's mother in that hall"

(b) hrēas blāc 2488a
he-fell pale
"he fell, pale"

Line (104a) is one of those excluded from consideration due to
lack of alliterating syllables. The hall of Grendel's mother is called
a *gūð-sele* "war-hall" in line 443a, and it seems likely that the
metrical defect in (104a) was caused by omission of *gūð-* or of
some other poetic combinative with the same metrical value (see
Dobbie 1953, 227). A combinative seems to have been dropped in
the second foot of (104b) as well. Klaeber is speculating when he
represents the poet's intention as *hrēas heoro-blāc:* The compound
could equally well have been *hilde-blac* "battle-bright."[12] Fortunately, a metrist need not decide among the possible alternatives.
From a theoretical point of view, what matters is that this exceptional pattern with two metrical positions could have resulted
from an expected *type* of scribal error.

In some compounds like *searo-gimmas* "treasure-jewels," both
constituents are vulnerable to omission. The *Beowulf* poet employs
searo-gimmas in descriptions of hoards that contain not only jewels
but other precious things as well, such as items of intricately crafted
military equipment. In these contexts, replacement of *searo-gimmas*
by *gimmas* "jewels" or by *searo* "treasure, armor" would create no
obvious semantic anomaly. Lines 3101–2 seem to show the scribe
dropping two constituents, one of which may have been the semantically inessential *-gimma* (genitive of *gimmas*):

(105) Uton nū efstan ōðre [sīðe]
let-us now hasten another time
"Let us now hurry back"

sēon ond sēcean searo[-gimma] geþræc
to-see and to-seek of-treasure-jewels a-heap
"to seek out a heap of jewels"

The bracketed constituents in (105), introduced by Klaeber, are
absent in the manuscript. No one regards 3101b as a legitimate

exception to metrical rules: *ōðre* supplies alliteration, but it makes no sense whatever without some such word as *sīðe*. Obviously, scribes did omit words, even when the effect on sense and meter was disastrous. Most editors assume that the lapse of attention responsible for 3101b continued through the following line, resulting in omission of a constituent there as well (see Dobbie 1953, 275–6).

Linguistic constituents matching the foot patterns Ssx, Sxs, or Sxxs can often be transformed into complete half-lines by the addition of an optional function word, which will provide the light foot for a type B or C pattern. Useful words for this purpose are definite articles, pronouns, and conjunctions, which the poet may add or omit with considerable freedom. In the restricted corpus of parallel verse texts, articles, pronouns, and conjunctions present in one manuscript are often missing in another. In manuscript B of *Solomon and Saturn*, for example, verse 288a reads *micles and mǣtes* "of high and low," where the corresponding verse in the A manuscript reads *micles, mǣtes*. Some editors conclude that the A scribe dropped a grammatically inessential *and* (see ASPR, vol. 6, 166).

A similar omission may have produced the following crux in *Beowulf*:

(106)   woldon (care) cwīðan, kyning mǣnan,
          they-would care tell, the-king mourn,
          "they wished to express their grief, mourn the king,

          word-gyd wrecan, ond ymb w(er) sprecan   3171–2
          word-saying to-utter, and about the-man to-speak
          to recite a eulogy and speak about the man"

Line 3172 exemplifies *sentence variation,* a type of artistic repetition whereby the poet alters the wording of an immediately preceding statement while retaining its syntax and meaning (see Robinson 1962, 21). Verse 3171b is unmetrical as it stands: obligatory resolution of the short stressed syllable in *kyning* leaves only enough linguistic material for three metrical positions. It seems unlikely that the poet would have employed *ond* in the variation while omitting *ond* in the preceding statement. One would expect the more compressed expression to occur last. Klaeber assumed that 3171b originally had *ond,* like 3172b. With *ond* restored, the verse qualifies as an instance of the type C pattern x//S/Sx.

The conjunction *ond,* usually represented by the Tironian sign for Latin *et (7),* is especially vulnerable to omission before words like *cyning,* which can be spelled with initial *c* or with initial *k.* The scribe places the Tironian sign very near to a following word, and the combination *7c* bears a rather close resemblance to *k* (compare lines 2144 and 2696 in the Zupitza-Davis facsimile, pp. 98, 125). Possibly *kyning* in the surviving manuscript reflects *7cyning* in the scribe's exemplar.[13]

Omission of unstressed function words also seems probable in two other exceptional verses:

(107) (a) grētte þā 652a
           greeted then
           "then greeted"

       (b) gegnum fōr 1404b
           ahead he-went
           "he went ahead"

All modern editors obtain a fourth metrical position by emending *grētte* of (107a) to the synonymous variant *gegrētte,* assuming that the scribe dropped the optional *ge-* prefix (compare *Azarias* 38a, which has *būgað* where the parallel text, *Daniel* 321a, has *bebūgað*). Klaeber emends (107b) to *swā gegnum fōr* "as he went ahead," and other editors also assume that one or more function words were dropped. With function words restored, (107a-b) qualify as instances of the type B pattern x/Sxs. As we noted above, a similar situation arises in verse 747b (96d), where the loss may have occurred through erasure.

In *Beowulf,* adjectives, determiners, and possessives normally precede their governed nouns, as in Old English prose. The poet employs noun-adjective word order with significant frequency, however, and verses like (32b, d) show an occasional use of the archaic noun-determiner construction to produce a simpler verse pattern. Archaic syntax seems to have created scribal confusion occasionally. Consider the following variants:

(108) (a)   yldran / ūsse (Azarias 18a)
            elders our
            "our elders"

      (b)   ūser / yldran (Daniel 297a)
            our elders
            "our elders"

Example (108a) corresponds to the simplest type A1 pattern Sx/
Sx, with *ūsse* receiving clause-final stress. In the *Daniel* text, the
scribe has apparently rejected the archaic word order preserved in
Azarias. Example (108b) has the more complex pattern xx/Sx,
with proclitic *ūser* occupying x positions.

The same type of alteration may have produced two very odd
lines in *Beowulf:*

(109) (a)   brūn-fāgne helm, hringde byrnan 2615
            bright-adorned helmet, ringed byrnie
            "bright helmet, ringed corslet"

      (b)   (hē is manna gehyld) hord openian 3056
            (he is men's protection) hoard to-open
            "(he is men's protection) to open the hoard"

In (109a-b), the first fully stressed word in the line, which occupies the strongest metrical position, fails to alliterate, violating
(50a). Line (109a) is doubly odd because the word that fails to
alliterate, *brūn-fāgne,* is a poetic compound. Several editors have
suggested that (109a-b) resulted from scribal normalization of the
poetic noun-adjective word order (see Dobbie 1953, 252, 271). If
hringde byrnan is emended to *byrnan hringde* and *manna gehyld*
is emended to *gehyld manna,* the verses have normal alliteration.

Most archaic forms employed by the *Beowulf* poet had been
replaced in ordinary speech by synonyms to which they bore no
formal resemblance. Thus archaic *wǣge* "cup" was replaced by
later forms like *full.* The scribe would not be likely to modernize
wǣge when it appeared in his exemplar, but the situation would
be different if the archaism bore a close resemblance to a later
form. In that case, the scribe might well assume that the old form
represented a more familiar form. Such a misunderstanding may
have produced an unmetrical verse in *Beowulf:*

(110) ealne ūtanweardne 2297a
       all outside
       "all outside"

Verse (110) would be acceptable in a hypermetrical cluster as an instance of the pattern Sx/Sxsx. Since (110) is not adjacent to another hypermetrical verse, however, it is generally regarded as unmetrical. A possible explanation for this anomaly involves the history of the noun *hlǣw* "burial mound," which appears in the preceding half-line. In surviving manuscripts, *hlǣw* usually follows the masculine paradigm, and the *-ne* endings of (110) show agreement with an accusative singular masculine *hlǣw* in 2996b. Earlier, though, *hlǣw* was a neuter *-es, -os* stem (see OEG, section 636). It seems possible that a neuter form existed in the poet's dialect or as an archaism in the traditional poetic diction. If so, (110) might reflect an original *eal ūtanweard* (cf. Dobbie 1953, 236). With neuter inflection, the verse conforms to the ordinary type Db pattern S/Sxs. The unmetrical (110) would have resulted when a scribe who interpreted *hlǣw* as masculine rejected the original half-line as ungrammatical.

Parallel verses with the same lexical items sometimes differ in grammatical construction. Here we have to deal with slight misunderstandings rather than with modernization. In the A manuscript of *Solomon and Saturn*, verse 76b, we find *ealra stāna gripe* "the weight of all stones" where manuscript B has *ealle stāna gripe* "all the weight of stones." The A scribe understood *eall* to modify genitive plural *stāna*, but the B scribe thought that it modified dative-instrumental singular *gripe*.

Two unmetrical verses in *Beowulf* may represent similar grammatical variants:

(111) (a) hilde-rinc 3124a
           battle-warrior
           "warrior"

      (b) ungedēfelīce 2435b   (alliteration on u-)
           unfittingly
           "in unseemly fashion"

Most editors assume that the three-position verse (111a) was originally *hilde-rinca,* genitive plural, dependent on *eahta* in the line preceding. Apparently the scribe interpreted *hilde-rinc* as the grammatical subject and altered its inflection accordingly (cf. Dobbie 1953, 277). Difference in meaning is slight: The poet probably intended "he went in a group of eight battle-warriors," but the scribal version asserts that "the battle-warrior went in a group of eight." In (111b), we find a pattern Sx/Sxsx without a hypermetrical partner, as in (110). Some textual critics emend to *ungedēfe,* an adjectival form that would modify *morþor-bed* "slaughter-bed" in the line below. The scribe seems to have added the adverbial suffix because he understood the word to modify past participle *strêd* "spread, prepared" (see Dobbie 1953, 241). Difference in meaning is again slight: under one interpretation, a bed of slaughter is prepared in unseemly fashion; according to the other reading, an unseemly bed of slaughter is prepared.

A related type of inflectional variant attested in parallel manuscripts involves the choice of one grammatical option rather than another. Verse 52a of *Solomon and Saturn* reads *heofona rīces* "of the kingdom of heaven," which has the simple type A1 pattern Sx/Sx. In the B text, we find the familiar compound *heofon-rīces* "of heaven-kingdom." Meaning is the same in each case, but since *heofon-* must be resolved, the B variant has only enough linguistic material to fill three metrical positions. A possible analogue in *Beowulf* is the following:

(112) þenden hē wið wulf 3027a
       when he with wolf
       "when he with the wolf"

Because Old English has no trisyllabic function words, there can be no four-position verse of the type xxx/S, and (112) must be declared unmetrical (cf. section 1.4). Here a peculiarity of Old English *wið* may have caused the scribal error. In the sense of "together with," *wið* governs dative or accusative (cf. *Beowulf* 1977–78, where one of two parallel *wið* phrases has a dative form and the other an accusative form). The scribe's accusative *wulf* probably reflects an original dative *wulfe* (see Dobbie 1953, 270). If so, (112) would qualify as an instance of the type A3 pattern (xx)xx/Sx, with the long string of unstressed syllables characteristic in this type.

10.4 The Metrist and the Editor

Since metrical analysis and textual criticism are often carried out simultaneously, it may be useful to emphasize that the discussion of exceptional verses above has metrical rather than editorial considerations in view. An editor who proposes an emendation must determine not only that the text is defective but also, to a high degree of probability, what the author intended. I have taken on the much easier task of showing that exceptions to the theory proposed here could well have resulted from scribal error. Of this I do not see how there can be any doubt. It seems clear that the psychological tendencies described above could have produced the number of exceptions encountered, or even more, to judge by surviving parallel texts. On the other hand, it is quite possible that some of the exceptional verses resulted from errors unlike those I have hypothesized.

10.5 Poetry and Prose

Any constraint on poetic form, whether metrical or grammatical, can help a text critic isolate problematic verses. A metrist is more particularly interested in distinguishing the language of a given poem from other varieties of language present in the poet's cultural milieu. Defining the difference between Old English poetry and Old English prose has proved particularly difficult due to the variety of attested verse patterns. Many clause patterns common in prose will satisfy the *Beowulf* poet's criteria for verses. Daunt (1947) went so far as to suggest that the *Beowulf* poet did not employ a poetic meter, but "the spoken language rather tidied up" (see Bessinger and Kahrl 1968, 296).

Comparison of *Beowulf* with a prose passage selected at random is somewhat problematic. To a considerable extent, the results will depend on how we choose to divide the prose sentences into units comparable with verses.[14] A more straightforward comparison can be carried out with the help of Aelfric's *Lives of Saints*. Pope (1967, 105) employs the term "rhythmical prose" to describe the diction of these works because they seem quite unlike *Beowulf* from a metrical point of view. On the other hand, Aelfric's use of alliteration makes it clear that he employed a meaningful line unit; and scribal "pointing" at the mid-line syntactic break indicates the presence of smaller significant units comparable to verses. To the extent that our theory identifies Aelfric's verse units as unmetrical, it captures what is poetic about the verses of *Beowulf*.

Aelfric's homily on the death of Saint Oswald is particularly useful for our purposes. A convenient text, fully glossed, appears in Cassidy and Ringler (1971, 240–9). The consistent employment of a mid-line syntactic break in this narrative allows the editors to divide it systematically into verse units. We will accept the editors' judgments in all cases, and will regard as verse units just what they print as verse units.

At the heart of our theory lies the claim that the simplest verses consist of two trochaic words. The *Beowulf* poet maintains a sense of the norm by favoring this pattern while restricting the frequency of more complex patterns. In the first 287 lines of *Beowulf* one can find over eighty verses consisting of two trochaic words with no extrametrical syllables (e.g. *hȳran scolde* 10b "should obey"). The 287 lines of Aelfric's narrative contain not a single such verse.

Aelfric does employ many verse units that contain trochaic words. The following, for example, would qualify as variants of Sievers type A1:

(113) (a)   (mid) lȳtlum / werode 15a
            with small troop
            "with a small troop"

   (b)   Aidan / (ge)hāten 53b
            Aidan called
            "named Aidan"

   (c)   ā tō / worulde 287a
            ever to eternity
            "forever and ever"

The high frequency of trochaic words in Old English will naturally produce "type A1" clauses like (113a-c) in all types of discourse. Yet it requires considerable effort to obtain a high frequency of verses like *hȳran scolde*. To produce such uncluttered verses in significant numbers, the poet must learn systematic procedures for deleting or relocating function words. The archaic syntax of traditional epic seems to play a significant role in freeing verses of extrametrical syllables. Rather than employing a verse like (113a), a traditional poet would use the archaic "dative of accompaniment" construction, in which the meaning "with" is expressed by the case ending (cf. *lītle weorode, Battle of Brunanburh* 34b; *lȳtle werede, Genesis* 2093b; *mǣte werede,* with the same meaning, *Dream of the Rood* 124a).

The Oswald narrative contains four half-lines like (113b) in which the form *gehāten* follows a bisyllabic personal name.[15] Similar half-lines in *Beowulf* employ instead a synonymous unprefixed form *hāten* (e.g. *Grendel hāten* 102b; cf. *Beowulf* 263b, 373b). The form *hāten* appears in poems as late as those of Aelfric. In *The Battle of Maldon,* for example, we find the verse *Ealhelm hāten* "named Ealhelm" (218b). If Aelfric's *gehāten* represents the colloquial norm, the use of *hāten* by more traditional poets would indicate a preference for verses free of extrametrical syllables.

Aelfric's half-lines do include some type A1 patterns with no extrametrical syllables. The one example in the Oswald narrative (113c) has a word group in the first foot, however. The more compact half-lines do not necessarily approximate norms emphasized by the *Beowulf* poet. Verse unit 70b consists of the single word *bodigende* "preaching," which can occupy only three metrical positions, since the first syllable is short. I do not see how the editors could be mistaken in representing *bodigende* as a verse unit. There is no other natural point of division in line 70, and the word following *bodigende,* a proclitic, must belong to line 71.

Among the shorter verse units in the Oswald narrative we find the following:

(114) (a) forð on his / weg 212b
       forth on his way
       "forth on his way"
       [Sxx/S]

   (b) sǣtan geond / (þā) strǣt 92b
       sat along the street
       "sat along the street"
       [Sxx/(x)S]

(c)   fērde wið / (þone) feld 204b
       went by that field
       "went by that field"
       [Sxx/(xx)S]

If the pattern Sxx/S arises so naturally for Aelfric, its extreme rarity in more traditional verse must be due to a strong metrical constraint. This consideration provides additional support for our rereading of (96e).

Let us now inspect the heavier verse units employed by Aelfric, those with three stressed syllables of the sort that occupy S or s positions obligatorily.[16] Once again comparison with *Beowulf* reveals striking differences. The first 287 lines of the epic contain more than seventy verses with three heavy stresses, including variants of Sievers types A2, D, and E. More than fifty verses consist of a compound accompanied by one other stressed word, with no extrametrical syllables. In the Oswald narrative we find a somewhat smaller number of verse units with three or more heavily stressed syllables, about sixty in all. There are *no* two-word expressions of types A2, D, or E corresponding to those in *Beowulf*. In fact, Aelfric's heavy verse units usually violate at least one of the categorical rules given above. Many violate two rules or even three.

About half of Aelfric's heavy verse units contain compounds of the most familiar type, corresponding to the foot pattern Ssx. A few of these have patterns resembling those attested in *Beowulf*:

(115) (a)   Gode / (tō) wurðmynte 18a, 44a
             to-God as praise
             "in praise of God"
             [S/(x)Ssx]

       (b)   þearfum / (and) wannhālum 276a
             to-needy and to-sick
             "to the needy and sick"
             [Sx/(x)Ssx]

       (c)   (of) sunnan / ūpgange 116a[17]
             of sun's up-going
             "from sunrise"
             [(x)Sx/Ssx]

(d) (and) blīðe / hām fērde 219b
and blithely home fared
"and went home happily"
[(x)Sx/Ssx]

The two verses with the pattern of (115a) would be acceptable in
Beowulf. The remaining verses might also be acceptable, though
their extrametrical words would render them quite complex. The
Beowulf poet employs non-prefixal extrametrical syllables very
seldom in heavy verses (see section 3.2).

Compounds of the form Ssx are subject to several constraints in
our theory. When such compounds appear in the first foot they
may not be preceded by extrametrical words (cf. (21a)), and the
second foot must contain a monosyllable or resolvable disyllable
(cf. (15b)). If an Ssx compound occupies the second foot, the first
foot may contain material sufficient to occupy one or two metrical
positions, but no more (cf. (13b)).

Aelfric makes no attempt to delete or relocate clause-initial
function words when he employs the reversed pattern Ssx/S. The
following verse unit is typical:

(116) (þone) wælhrēowan / cynincg 42b
the slaughter-cruel king
"the slaughterous king"
[(xx)Ssx/S]

Like (116) are 31a, 107a, 111b, 144b, 207b, 269b, 270a, and
278a.

Aelfric seems equally unconcerned about constraints on the
number of metrical positions in reversed patterns:

(117) (a) untrumra / manna 32a   (alliteration on u-)
of-unsound men
"of unsound men"
[Ssx/Sx]

(b) Ōswoldes / cynerīce 104a
Oswald's kingdom
"Oswald's kingdom"
[Sxx/Ssx]

137

(c) wanhālum / (tō) þicgenne 202b
     for-unsound to receive
     "for unsound people to receive"
     [Ssx/(x)Sxx]

(d) (þǣre) dēorwurðan / stōwe 223b
     of-the dear-worth place
     "of the blessed place"
     [(xx)Ssx/Sx]

(e) (and mid) wurðmynte / gelōgode 142b
     and with honor deposited
     "and deposited with honor"
     [(xx)Ssx/(x)Sxx]

Example (117a) constitutes a reversed pattern of the sort forbidden by (15b), with five metrical positions. Example (117b) violates rule (13b), which states that only one foot may have three metrical positions. Example (117c) violates both (13b) and (15b). Violation of constraints on the number of metrical positions is aggravated in (117d-e) by violation of constraints on extrametrical syllables (cf. verse units 20a, 36b, 53a, 216b, and 276b).

We also note some violations of (13b) and (15b) involving word groups with the pattern S/Sx:

(118) (a) Godes / willan // (ge)fremman 125b
           God's will to-perform
           "to do God's will"
           [S/Sx//(x)Sx]

      (b) (embe) Godes / willan // (tō) smēagenne 45b
           about God's will to think
           "to meditate about God's will"
           [(xx)S/Sx//(x)Sxx]

Note that (118a-b) do not qualify as hypermetrical verses because the major constituent break falls after the second stressed word (cf. section 6.3).

We next consider a few verse units with compounds of the form Sxs or word groups of the form Sx/S. One of these units bears a certain resemblance to expanded type Db:

Rules and Exceptions

(119) (þæs) cyninges // swȳþran / hand 99a
the king's right hand
"the king's right hand"
[(x)Sx//Sx/S]

Note, however, that the extrametrical word in verse-initial position is an article rather than a prefix. There is nothing like (119) in *Beowulf,* and this half-line may in fact be unacceptably complex.

Categorical violations occur when the pattern Sxs or Sx/S appears in first position:

(120) (a) (ac þā) mynstermenn / noldon 179a[18]
but the minster-men would-not
"but the monks would not"
[(xx)Sxs/Sx]

(b) (þæt hē) hālig / sanct // wæs 182b[19]
that he a-holy saint was
"that he was a holy saint"
[(xx)Sx/S//S]

Example (120a) seems to exhaust the possibilities of unmetricality, violating (15a), (15b), and (21a). Example (120b) violates (15a) and (21a). Note that the positioning of constituent breaks in (120b) forces assignment of the noun phrase *hālig sanct* to the first foot (cf. (118a-b)).

Only two verse units in the Oswald narrative contain constituents of the form Ss or S/S:

(121) (a) (swilce) hēalic / sunnbēam 184b
like a-bright sunbeam
"like a bright sunbeam"
[(xx)Sx/Ss]

(b) Godes / lof // (ā)rǣrende 137a
God's praise raising
"offering up praise to God"
[S/S//(x)Sxx]

Example (121a) might be acceptable as a variant of type A2, but the anacrusis would render it more complex than any member of

139

its type attested in *Beowulf*. A b-verse of this sort is of course wholly unacceptable if we take into account rule (29), which restricts complexity in the second half-line. Example (121b) violates the constraint against supernumerary metrical positions in verses with a compound or heavy word group in first position (15b).

Two verse units in the Oswald narrative bear some resemblance to the hypermetrical verses of *Beowulf*:

(122) (a)   (and) twēgen / (his) æftergengan 10a
            and two his successors
            "and two of his successors"
            [(x)Sx/(x)Sxsx]

      (b)   God, // (ge-)miltsa / (ūrum) sāwlum 161b
            God, have-mercy on-our souls
            "God, have mercy on our souls"
            [S//(x)Sx/(xx)Sx]

Example (122a) is a valid hypermetrical pattern with a type of anacrusis attested in *Beowulf* (cf. 1166a). In cases like (122b), where the third S position is occupied by a fully stressed word, the *Beowulf* poet would require double alliteration (cf. section 8.7). This verse unit bears a certain resemblance to a hypermetrical a-verse; but as a b-verse, it would be totally out of place. Neither (122a) nor (122b) is adjacent to another hypermetrical pattern, and both can therefore be said to violate the overlap constraint (12).

In traditional Old English poetry, the overlapping feet of hypermetrical verses always appear in second position, like complex feet of the form Sxs or Sxxs. Aelfric typically locates overlapping feet in first position, and often precedes them with extrametrical words:

(123) (a)   ūpāwendum / handbredum 118a[20]
            with-upturned palms
            "with upturned palms"
            [Sxsx/Ssx]

      (b)   (and ge-)rihtlǣcende / (þæt) folc 137b[21]
            and directing that people
            "and directing that people"
            [(xx)Ssxx/(x)S]

(c) eahta / (and) þrittig // gēare 149b
    eight and thirty years
    "thirty-eight years"
    [Sx/(x)Sx//Sx]

(d) (on) Sancte / Pētres // mynstre 173b[22]
    in Saint Peter's minster
    "in Saint Peter's minster"
    [(x)Sx/Sx//Sx]

Example (123a) shows an overlapping foot of the form Sxsx in first position. In (123b) and six other verses, the overlapping foot is preceded by unstressed syllables in anacrusis. Example (123c) shows a heavy word group occupying the overlapping foot. Note that the position of the major constituent break precludes analysis of (123c) as an instance of the pattern Sx//(x)Sx/Sx. Verse units resembling (123c) contain initial unstressed words more often than not. Example (123d) is typical.

From the standpoint of a theory that relates feet to words, Aelfric contrasts with the *Beowulf* poet in every significant respect. Two-word norms emphasized by the *Beowulf* poet are nowhere to be found in the Oswald narrative. Deviations from two-word norms unattested in the traditional epic are in Aelfric's work everywhere apparent. Aelfric simply does not employ "feet," in the sense here defined.

Those of Aelfric's verse units that scan as type B or C have a very peculiar distribution, viewed from the perspective of traditional verse.[23] In *Beowulf*, the balanced pattern that predominates is the type C pattern with a second foot of the form Ssx (or S/Sx, with the substitution of S for s allowed by (68a)). I found somewhat more than 980 total occurrences, excluding verses in which the second foot could be analyzed as Sxx. Next in frequency are the ordinary type B patterns with a second foot of the form Sxs (or Sx/S). There are somewhat less than 860 of these in the poem. The long type B variants with a second foot of the form Sxxs (or Sxx/S) have a much lower frequency: less than 170 total occurrences. In the Oswald narrative I found only 15 verse units analyzable as type C (excluding again those with a second foot of the form Sxx). There were 36 of the ordinary type B verses, and no less than 30 with the long type B pattern.

Since Aelfric is not restricted by the rules of traditional verse, his balanced patterns presumably occur with something like their natural frequency. The distribution of balanced patterns in *Beowulf* would then indicate the presence of metrical restrictions. Within the theory proposed here, we can explain these differences between traditional verse and "rhythmical prose" by reference to principles I and II, which state that foot patterns corresponding to familiar word patterns are relatively easy to perceive, while foot patterns corresponding to unusual word patterns add to complexity. Verse types with a second foot of the form Sxxs are obviously useful, since they correspond to many syntactic structures employed as verse units by Aelfric; but the rarity of words like *sib-begedriht* means that traditional verses containing the Sxxs foot will be difficult to analyze. Hence the artificially restricted number of long type B patterns in *Beowulf*. Balanced patterns of type C correspond to syntactic structures that occur relatively seldom in Aelfric's narrative, and would therefore seem to be less "useful" than the type B patterns. The high frequency of type C verses in *Beowulf* can be explained by reference to the simplicity of the foot pattern Ssx, which corresponds to the most familiar compound pattern.

In verses containing three stressed words, (3b) requires assignment of stressed words to feet in accordance with syntactic constituency. The foot boundary of a typical heavy verse like (4) falls at the major constituent break, and the word group occupying the second foot has a syntactic integrity much like that of a compound word. In the simpler patterns with two stressed constituents, the foot boundary does not always occur at the most natural syntactic location (though it must, of course, coincide with a word boundary). The major constituent break of a type B or C verse can fall between the stressed constituents of the second foot rather than between the first foot and the second. Although type B and C verses with unnatural syntax are tolerated, we would expect traditional poets to regard them as complex, and to restrict their numbers accordingly. The strength of the traditional poet's bias can be estimated by comparing the frequency of such verses in *Beowulf* with their frequency in Aelfric's rhythmical prose.

Consider the following verse units, which resemble the balanced patterns of *Beowulf*:

Rules and Exceptions

(124) (a)   Hē / (wolde æfter) ūht-sange 114a
he would after evensong
"after evensong, he was accustomed"
[x/(xxxx)Ssx]

(b)   binnan // twām / gēarum 10b
within two years
"within two years"
[xx//S/Sx]

(c)   (þider hē) ge- / mynt hæfde 213a
where he intended had
"where he had intended (to go)"
[(xxx)x/Ssx]

(d)   Sēo / (ylce) rōd siððan 30a
the same rood afterwards
"afterwards, the same cross"
[x/(xx)Ssx]

(e)   (swā swā) sum / mæsseprēost 241a
as some mass-priest
"as a certain priest"
[(xx)x/Sxs]

(f)   wiþ // heofones / weard 118b
toward heaven's guardian
"toward God"
[x//Sx/S]

(g)   ā- / fyrhte āweg 231b
frightened away
"away, being frightened"
[x/Sxxs, or x/Sxs with elision]

(h)   (þæt) his / earm tōbærst 34b
so-that his arm broke
"so that his arm was broken"
[(x)x/Sxs]

Verse unit (124a) can be analyzed as a simple variant of type C, with a compound occupying the second foot. In (124b), the second foot is occupied by a word group, but the foot boundary falls in the most natural location, at the major constituent break. From the standpoint of traditional meter, example (124c) is complex, since the syntactic relation between *ge-* and *-mynt* is closer than that between *-mynt* and *hæfde*. The same sort of complexity can be seen in (124d), where *ylce* is more closely linked to *rōd* than is *rōd* to *siððan*. Examples (124e-h) show comparable gradations of complexity in verse units analyzable as type B, with (124e-f) representing the simple variants and (124g-h) representing the complex variants.

We observed above that our corpus contains 15 verse units analyzable as type C if we exclude from consideration those with a second foot of the form Sxx. Of these, 6, or 40%, fall into the "complex" category represented by (124c-d). The corresponding figure for *Beowulf* is 23%. The contrast with respect to type B verses is equally sharp, and perhaps more significant, since a larger sample of type B verse units is available for inspection. Of 66 such verse units in the Oswald narrative, 38, or about 58%, fall into the complex category (cf. (124g-h)). The corresponding figure for *Beowulf* is 32%. If the statistics from the Oswald narrative are reliable, they indicate that the *Beowulf* poet restricted complex variants of balanced patterns to just slightly more than half of their natural frequency. In section 1.5.2, we noted that the complex variants of types B and C correspond most closely to the patterns xS/xS and xS/Sx posited by Sievers. Our decision to reject such patterns is motivated in part by the fact that there are no genuinely iambic words native to Old English which could serve as prototypes for an xS foot (cf. section 1.1.1 and section 1.4). Statistical considerations provide additional support for this decision. It seems clear that half-lines like (124c-d) and (124g-h) were interpreted as mismatches – allowable, but complex – to patterns with a heavy foot in second position.

The comparison with Aelfric should leave us once again with considerable respect for the *Beowulf* poet. The variety of patterns in the epic may suggest prose at first glance; but these patterns are weighed, measured, and distributed according to very strict standards. The poet's "tidying up" of the spoken language is anything but casual. Nothing we call "meter" has a clearer right to that distinction.

11

OVERVIEW

≈ ≈

11.1 Fundamental Principles

We have found no reason to modify our assumption that metrical feet correspond to words or our assumption that alliterative patterns correspond to stress patterns. On the contrary, refinements such as (66) and (68) result from a stricter interpretation of principles I and III than seemed possible at first. Nor have we compromised the "numerical" component of the theory that defines a verse as a pair of feet and a line as a pair of verses. This component of the theory now applies to hypermetrical patterns as well as to normal patterns (cf. section 8.8). Reduced to its essentials, the theory consists of principles I-IV. The more concrete rules merely serve to implement these principles, and do not count as independent assumptions.

11.2 Rules

The principle that foot patterns correspond to word patterns is implemented by several rules (refer to Appendix). These impose constraints on deviation from the ideal foot, which contains a single word. Labeling rules (2a-c), simplified later in (66), require that each foot should be quite "word-like" with regard to its stress pattern. Syllables with primary stress must always occupy S positions and syllables with zero stress must always occupy x positions. A foot may contain only one unsubordinated metrical position: When two syllables of primary stress appear within the foot, the S position occupied by the second must undergo metrical subordination to the S position occupied by the first (cf. (47), (68)). Bracketing rule (3a) requires that every foot boundary must correspond to a word boundary. Rule (3b) requires that assignment of stressed words to feet in heavy verses must take account of natural constituent breaks. The severe restrictions imposed by labeling and bracketing rules ensure that any word group occupying the foot will be recognizable as an "artificial word." Many verse forms allow for varying metrical interpretation of words with a complex or ambiguous phonological makeup (cf. Kiparsky, 1968, 1972). In Old English meter, we have the prosodic rules governing interpretation of vowel contraction (24) and epenthesis (26), together with the metrical rule of resolution (27), which governs interpretation of short stressed syllables.

Principle II posits an ideal verse consisting of two trochaic words. Rules that implement principle II take the form of constraints on deviation from this ideal. Many types of deviation occur. One finds verses with extrametrical words and verses with supernumerary metrical positions. The poet may employ feet much larger or smaller than the standard foot, and may choose to thwart audience expectations with regard to the positioning of compound foot patterns. The limits of deviation, however, are quite definite. Only compound feet corresponding to the more familiar compound word patterns may appear in the less usual location (cf. (15a)). The unexpected positioning of a compound foot within a given verse precludes the employment in that verse of supernumerary metrical positions (cf. (15b)) or of anacrusis (cf. (21a)). Employment of short feet may not produce verse patterns with fewer than the normal number of syllables (cf. (13a)). A normal verse may contain only one long foot (cf. (13b)). Employment of very long "overlapping" feet in hypermetrical verses is allowed only when "clustering" signals a shift from one metrical subsystem to the other (cf. (12), (38)). A hypermetrical verse may contain only one overlapping foot, which must appear in second position, like a complex normal foot of the form Sxs or Sxxs.

In addition to categorical constraints forbidding simultaneous deviation, we can detect other constraints orchestrating the relative frequencies of verses with allowable types of deviation (discussed in Chapter 5). Since frequency statistics are affected by a number of nonmetrical factors, there was no reason to expect such clear-cut results. The relative frequencies may be especially informative because of the *Beowulf* poet's fondness for metrical variety, which entails a systematic exploitation of the rarer patterns right up to the limits imposed by their complexity.

Complex verses will not threaten the sense of a norm if the poet is careful to reiterate the simpler types with a higher relative frequency. The restriction on complexity in the second half-line (29) also helps to emphasize the simpler patterns.

Principles III and IV link alliteration to stress. The rules implementing these principles are of two types, those that refer directly to linguistic material and those that refer to metrical patterns abstracted from linguistic material. Rules of the first type specify what kind of syllable may alliterate. Such a syllable normally has linguistic prominence within its clause, and must always bear some degree of stress (cf. (50c) and section 9.12). Rules of the second type determine what metrical positions may or must contain alliterating syllables. The metrical subordination rule assigns relative prominence to the first of two S positions when both lie within the same domain, mimicking the Old English compound stress rule (cf. (47), (68a)). Rules (50a-d) and (68b) mark the most prominent metrical positions in the line for alliteration. Every line pattern can be regarded as a kind of giant word in which relations of prominence result from application of the Old English compound stress rule. As in other meters, the coherence of the line results from application of a word-level rule outside its normal domain (cf. Kuryłowicz 1970, 7). The matching rules of (2), which permit assignment of any stressed syllable to a prominent metrical position, explain the occasional alliteration of weakly stressed syllables in verses where an accompanying syllable of stronger stress fails to alliterate.

The rules defining metrical patterns make no mention of alliteration, but provide just the right domains for application of (47), (50a-d), and (68a-b). Since this meshing of theoretical subcomponents could hardly result from chance, it seems reasonable to claim that the alliterative rules provide independent support for a word-based concept of the foot.

11.3 Acquisition of Poetic Rules

A metrical system must be "simple" enough, in some appropriate sense of the word, to make learning possible under ordinary conditions. The number of rules that implement principles I-IV may seem somewhat large, but the coherence of the metrical system and its grounding in preexisting cognitive capacities would have minimized learning difficulty. I take it as given that a competent poet can determine almost instantly, without conscious effort, whether a given string of words qualifies as a realization of an acceptable verse pattern. Yet we cannot conclude from the ease of such a calculation that it involved only two or three steps, or that the steps involved should be easy to discover. Theoretical linguists frequently find it necessary to warn against confusion between rule-governed *behavior,* which takes place unconsciously, and a system of rules *explaining* that behavior (cf. Lightfoot 1982, 20– 1). Scientific rules that represent our intuitions are seldom intuitively obvious, and it can require a great deal of effort to formulate them properly (when we can formulate them at all). We need not learn linguistics to learn how to speak – in fact, no one has ever done so. If the apprehension of metrical form draws on specialized cognitive capacities that facilitate analysis of linguistic material, as seems likely, the poet could acquire a rather complex set of metrical constraints by intuition, without conscious awareness of the details. Metrists should be prepared to discover systems with a moderate number of rules that relate norms to utterances.

11.4 Metrical Complexity in the Work of Master Poets

Certain familiar beliefs about what constitutes good poetry tend to support the hypothesis of an indirect relation between metrical norms and actual verses. Consider the pejorative term "singsong." It would be hard to find a native speaker of English interested in poetry who did not know this term. Yet what exactly does it imply? It seems quite certainly to imply that linguistic material *should not* always realize the norm. Daunt (1947) can imagine no greater form of torture "than to listen, night after night, to a story set in the meter of *Hiawatha*" (Bessinger and Kahrl 1968, 293; cf. Kiparsky 1977, 224). Narrative poets are supposed to find ways of providing metrical variety while maintaining the clear sense of a norm that stamps their work as poetic. The *Beowulf* poet's search for variety manifests itself as a determination to exploit all possible two-foot patterns while allowing for employment of word groups within the foot. The rule system defines the point at which this determination confronts the limits of metrical coherence.

Overview

There is of course no simple explanation for the fact that the limits of metrical coherence lie just where they do. To provide such an explanation we would probably have to know a good deal more about human cognitive capacities than we know at present. Here I have simply tried to show that the patterns avoided by the poet require more analytical effort than do those employed freely.

What seems clear is that good poets and appreciative audiences have a remarkable ability to identify complex verses as variants of regular patterns. It is this ability that interests linguists most, since it represents a kind of intuitive linguistic work. Both linguists and poets begin with a set of internalized grammatical concepts that apply in normal language use. Both must then learn to problematize these concepts from new perspectives. Some researchers may find it difficult to acknowledge an epic poet as a colleague or rival. Yet we must admit that such poets exercise artistic control over aspects of language resistant to systematic explanation. Everyone knows, for example, that literary artists produce intricately ordered narratives. Yet linguistics is at present unable to explain the structure of the simplest folktale in any truly scientific way. Those who attempted to devise a formal science of "discourse analysis" during the postwar years vastly underestimated the difficulty of the problem (cf. Chomsky 1968, 2–4). We should not be too confident of our knowledge even in the comparatively well-defined area of phonology. Advances in phonology have undoubtedly deepened our insight into poetic form, but no theory of meter can be definitive at present. Further progress in our understanding of language will undoubtedly suggest ways to improve the theory proposed here.

APPENDIX: RULE SUMMARY

Fundamental Principles (section 0.2)

Principle I: *Foot patterns* correspond to native Old English word patterns. The foot patterns most easily perceived are those that correspond to the most common word patterns.

Principle II: The *verse* consists of two feet. Foot patterns corresponding to unusual word patterns add to the complexity of verses in which they appear.

Principle III: *Alliterative patterns* correspond to Old English stress patterns. A metrical rule that mimics the Old English compound stress rule determines the location of alliterating syllables.

Principle IV: The *line* consists of two adjacent verses with an acceptable alliterative pattern.

Definition of "Word" (section 1.1.4)

A. All stressed simplexes count as words.
B. Unstressed prefixes count as "function words."
C. A compound may count as one word or as two.
D. A "function word" may count as a word or as undefined linguistic material.

Definition of Metrical Positions (section 1.3)

A. Fully stressed syllables generate S positions.
B. Syllables with secondary stress generate s positions.
C. Syllables with less than secondary stress generate x positions.

Appendix

Matching Rules

(2) (a) A syllable with primary stress may occupy an S position or (under certain conditions) an s position [revised in (66)].

(b) A syllable with zero stress must occupy an x position.

(c) A syllable with secondary stress may occupy an s position or (under certain conditions) an S position [cf. (3a-b)].

(3) (a) Every foot boundary must coincide with a word boundary. Note: The internal boundaries of compounded forms count as "word boundaries" for the purposes of this rule.

(b) In verses with three or more stressed words, the stressed words are assigned to feet in accordance with their syntactic constituency. Note: Compounds count as two words for the purposes of this rule.

Verse Pattern Rules

(12) Foot patterns may not overlap verse patterns [except as allowed by (38)].

(13) (a) A short foot must be paired with a long foot.

(b) Only one foot may be long.

(15) (a) Reversed half-line patterns may not contain a foot of the form Sxs or Sxxs.

(b) Reversed half-line patterns may not exceed normative length.

Extrametrical Word Rules

(21) (a) Unstressed words may appear before either foot, except before the first foot of a reversed half-line or before the first foot of a verse pattern wholly occupied by a compound.

(b) Extrametrical words reduce complexity in verse patterns with a light foot and add to complexity in verse patterns with an S position in the first foot. Note: When the first foot contains an S position, extrametrical syllables in anacrusis cause more complexity than do extrametrical syllables before the second foot.

Rules for Metrical Variants

(24)   PR1 (optional)
       Disregard the rule of vowel contraction.

(26)   PR2 (optional)
       Disregard the rule of epenthesis.

(27) (a) A short syllable bearing primary stress normally undergoes resolution.

   (b) A short syllable on an S position normally undergoes resolution.

   (c) When more than one metrical position in a verse may contain a resolved sequence, resolution is obligatory on the first such position.

Principle of Closure

(29)   Minimize complexity in the second half-line.

Hypermetrical Verse Rule

(38)   The second foot of a hypermetrical verse overlaps a normal verse pattern with an S position in the first foot.

Rules for Alliteration

(47)   When two constituents containing S positions appear within the same metrical domain, label the first constituent strong and the second constituent weak.

Appendix

(50) (a) The strongest two metrical positions within the line must contain alliterating syllables.

  (b) A weak constituent of a weak constituent may not contain an alliterating syllable.

  (c) No alliterating syllable may occupy an x position.

  (d) Otherwise, alliteration is optional.

Metrical Compounding within the Foot

(68) (a) Assignment of metrical stress to the first constituent of a small foot pair creates a higher-level foot.

  (b) A constituent receiving metrical stress must contain an alliterating syllable.

(76) Poetic compounds count as two words.

NOTES

1 A raised dot indicates the boundary between half-lines in a number of Old English poetic manuscripts. With respect to such "pointing" in the *Beowulf* manuscript, see Dobbie (1953, xxx). The domains isolated by pointing have a considerable degree of syntactic integrity. Editors of *Beowulf* assume, for example, that half-lines do not end with proclitic words such as conjunctions, articles, and prepositions. Exceptions to this rule are few and doubtful (see OEG, sections 97–99).

2 The first half of the line is called the *a-verse* or *on-verse*. The notation 254a indicates the a-verse of line 254. The second half-line is called the *b-verse* or *off-verse*. The partner of 254a would be called 254b. Transcription of verses cited from *Beowulf* is based on the edition of Klaeber (1950). I occasionally suppress Klaeber's punctuation or diacritical marks, and I often hyphenate compounds for clarity of exposition. Other verse citations are taken from the ASPR (Krapp and Dobbie 1931–53), with indications of vowel length added where appropriate. My first priorities in translating have been accurate representation of syntax and morphology. Problems of meaning will be discussed only where they have some bearing on the argument.

3 A syllable is long if it contains a long vowel (indicated by a macron) or a short vowel followed by one or more consonants. Within the word, a single consonant between vowels belongs to the following syllable rather than to the preceding syllable. A single consonant at the end of a word makes the last syllable long, however. The spellings *ēa, ēo, īe, īo* represent "long diphthongs" equivalent in length to long vowels; the spellings *ea, eo, ie, io* represent "short diphthongs" equivalent to short vowels (see OEG, sections 37–9).

4 Nouns, adjectives, infinitives, and participles are generally regarded as having the most prominent sentence stress. A few systematic exceptions are discussed in section 9.9.

5 The most influential discussions of unmetrical patterns are those in Sievers (1885, 1893); Pope (1942); Bliss (1958); and Cable (1974).

6 The concepts "internalized grammar" and "word pattern" have been made familiar by the tradition of generative phonology that begins with Chomsky and Halle (1968). Researchers working within this tradition assume that the human language learner can acquire intuitively, without conscious effort, rule systems of considerable abstractness and complexity. Acquisition of complex metrical systems can take place intuitively because the learner is able to draw on preexisting intuitive knowledge. Jakobson (1963) discusses intuitive learning of grammatical and metrical rules by illiterate Yugoslavian bards (see Jakobson 1979, 195–6). For further discussion, see sections 11.3–4 below.

7 The word-final -m in grim closes the syllable and makes it long. Hence grim ond is equivalent to gomban.

8 This view seems quite popular in comprehensive surveys of English meter. For criticism of such surveys, see Cable (1974, 8).

9 Jakobson (1979, 576) complains about this attitude in particularly strong terms, claiming that it has yielded no significant results.

10 Halle and Keyser (1971) are exceptional in this regard.

11 See Jespersen (1924, 92); Jakobson (1979, 576).

12 The canonical English pentameter poets frequently split simplex words with the foot boundary (i.e., they include part of the simplex within one foot while including another part of the simplex within an adjacent foot). I shall argue below that this type of mismatch never occurs in Old English verse. The large number of foot patterns in the Old English metrical system makes it possible to confine every type of simplex within the boundaries of a single foot.

NOTES TO CHAPTER I

1 The bond between true prefixes and root syllables is weaker than that between the constituents of compounds (see for example Kuryłowicz 1975, 6). Old English prefixes differ significantly from certain constituents sometimes confused with prefixes, such as the pre- in Modern English words like prepare. Since -pare does not occur as a separable word, pre- must be regarded as part of a simplex in this case. Pre- is a true prefix only in forms like pre-verbal, where the second constituent can occur in isolation. Sometimes word-level sound change rules indicate the difference between a true

prefix and an old prefix incorporated into a simplex. In *executive, exact,* and *exude,* for example, /ks/ voices to [gz]; but this word-level rule does not apply in forms like *ex-educator, ex-actor,* or *ex-Utah congressman.*

Even true Modern English prefixes are less word-like than are Old English prefixal elements. Constituents such as *pre-* and *ex-* do not resemble separable words, but most Old English prefixes show an obvious kinship with separable prepositions or adverbs. Many of our native prefixes have now lost their independent status. In Old English, the *be-* of *behealdan* is clearly related to the preposition *be,* but the *be-* of Modern English *behold* can hardly be related synchronically to the preposition *by.*

2 In early versions of generative phonology, the concept "word" was treated in a somewhat artificial fashion (see for example the tentative discussion of the subject in Chomsky and Halle 1968, 366–72). The "lexical phonology" approach employs a more natural concept of "word" (see Kiparsky 1982). Rules of lexical phonology apply simultaneously with derivational processes. Some rules are restricted to "stage I morphology" (i.e. to simplexes), while others apply only at "later" stages (e.g. within derived words or at the level of the sentence). Particularly interesting from our point of view is Kiparsky's level of "phrase phonology" intermediate between "word-level phonology" and "full-fledged sentence phonology" (p. 144). If Old English forms with prefixes properly belonged to this intermediate level, it is easy to see why they might count as two separate "words."

3 Bauer (1983, section 3.3.5) shows the futility of trying to establish rigid criteria for distinguishing between "lexicalized" words and "non-lexicalized" words. Many compounds are lexicalized in one way (e.g. semantically) but not in others (e.g. phonologically).

4 I use "x position" as shorthand for the cumbersome expression "a weak position within the metrical pattern or an extrametrical position." We have to reckon with extrametrical *positions* because the number of extrametrical syllables is restricted under certain conditions. Extrametrical syllables are free of constraints on metrical patterns, but obey special laws of their own (formulated in Chapter 3).

5 Reduced stress is thought to have been present in the secondary constituents of semantically lexicalized compounds, notably proper names; in certain suffixes; and in certain unsyncopated medial syllables (see OEG, sections 87–92). I do not wish to make any strong claims about the *acoustic* properties of syllables with "reduced stress." Their acoustic realization may in fact have alternated between that characteristic of unreduced secondary constituents in compounds and that characteristic of inflectional endings. For our

purposes, it is sufficient to observe that syllables with "reduced stress" behave in some respects like syllables with "secondary stress" and in other respects like syllables with "zero stress." The question of acoustic realization, now very controversial, is discussed below in sections 7.6, 8.5, and 9.1.

Note that in a metrical theory deriving feet directly from words it is unnecessary to take a strong position on acoustic realization of syllables. The theory could be reformulated in such a way that metrical positions were derived from morphological constituents. I use the terms "primary stress," "secondary stress," "reduced stress," and "zero stress" to identify natural classes of syllables, not to endorse any particular theory of stress levels. Instead of e.g. "zero stress" one might read "whatever property is common to inflectional endings and conjunctions like *ond.*"

6 Possibly some syllables of reduced stress were those shifting from secondary stress to zero stress in forms undergoing lexicalization. If so, we might allow such forms to generate two patterns, one corresponding to the earlier pronunciation with secondary stress and another corresponding to the lexicalized pronunciation with zero stress. The two pronunciations might sometimes coexist within the poet's linguistic milieu. To take a present example from my own environment: The type of portable radio with headphones called a "Walkman" is pronounced by some people with zero stress on the second constituent (cf. *chairman*), but with unreduced [mæn] by others (cf. *mailman*).

7 The reader may notice that large inflected forms like *middangeardes* are missing from the list. These are discussed in section 2.3 below.

8 Lack of stress has reduced most Old English function words to a single syllable, though some forms with two syllables exist (e.g. *ofer* "over"). In languages with strong phrasal stress, a trisyllabic unstressed word is practically a contradiction in terms. It is worth noting that all verse-initial trisyllabic words employed by the *Beowulf* poet alliterate. As we shall see in Chapter 9, such alliteration signals the presence of a significant stress.

9 The compounding process strips off inflectional endings in most cases. Hence the first constituent of a compound usually consists of a stressed monosyllable or a resolvable sequence. Compounds like *middangeard,* in which the first constituent has a trochaic pattern, are distinctly in the minority. Compounds like *sibbegedriht,* with a trochaic first constituent and an unstressed infix, are rarer still.

10 Early Irish alliterative poets can maintain a half-line of two words, but their brief poems usually consist of isolated phrases in asyndetic parataxis (see Travis 1973, 1–14; Murphy 1961, 3–7). If this Irish

meter was ever used for narrative purposes, it must have been more tolerant on occasion of verses with more than one word per foot.

11 These rules apply to short stressed syllables in the same way as to long stressed syllables. Note, however, that the short stressed syllable occupying an S or s position will sometimes share that position with the unstressed syllable of the resolvable sequence.

12 Although syllables with reduced stress *may* occupy S positions, they do so in relatively few cases. I discuss some examples in section 9.2.

13 It follows that a large compound like *middan-geardes* can constitute a whole verse (cf. section 2.3 below). Note that although a foot boundary must always coincide with a word boundary, not all word boundaries need coincide with foot boundaries (i.e., word groups are allowed within the foot).

14 Hence, in a verse consisting of a compound and a stressed simplex, the compound occupies one foot and the stressed simplex occupies the other. No foot can contain a stressed word and part of a compound.

15 Two apparent exceptions, which may be otherwise explained, are discussed below in sections 8.6 and 10.2.

16 The nonradical syllables of *ancre* and *rixode* bear no resemblance whatever to independent words, and one cannot therefore motivate an internal word boundary in these forms. The situation is different in forms like *ellen-līce* "bold-fashion, boldly" (discussed in section 9.2 below).

17 If unstressed prefixes count as function words, of course, verses with the structure of (7a) or (8a) all have more than two words, and cannot serve as prototypes for verse patterns. Unusual verses like (8a) are more common than those like (7a) because the simpler type C pattern is more tolerant of additional complexity (cf. sections 2.5 and 3.5). For more evidence supporting our reanalysis of types B and C, see section 10.5.

18 The requirement that extrametrical words must stand *before* the foot amounts to a restriction against extrametrical words in verse-final position. Any unstressed syllables lying between two verse patterns belong to the following verse pattern, and must obey the constraints on extrametrical syllables for that pattern (specified below in (21)).

19 The notation is that made familiar by Klaeber (1950, 281) and Creed (1966, 26). "Dax" stands for "expanded Da" and "Dbx" stands for "expanded Db."

20 I assume that *oncȳð* underwent lexicalization at some point in its history and may be interpreted as metrical Sx rather than as metrical Ss. This assumption is supported by forms such as *oncȳð-dǣd* "injurious deed" (*Andreas* 1179b). The Old English compounding process

operates on two familiar preexisting forms. When we find a compound as the first constituent of another compound, some degree of lexicalization in the embedded compound is implied (cf. section 7.4). Weakening or loss of stress is especially likely to occur when the root syllable in the subordinated constituent stands at the end of the word (OEG, section 88). The poet is careful to employ compound patterns in the first foot only when the verse has the normal number of metrical positions (see section 2.5). Since Ss never appears as the first foot of a pattern with five metrical positions, it would be surprising to find Ss as the first foot of a pattern with six metrical positions.

21 It goes without saying that no compound can have more than one secondary constituent. The relative prominence of tertiary constituents in forms like *in-wit-net* is discussed below (section 7.4).

1   When a poet repeats the same verse pattern several times in succession, the more complex variants of the pattern are easy to recognize as analogues of the simpler variants. An Old Irish "run" cited by Travis (1973, 12) is particularly instructive. Twelve verses in the run consist of a trochaic word followed by a stressed monosyllable. In the middle of the run, however, we find a verse consisting of a monosyllabic stressed word followed by an "iambic" word with an unstressed prefix. The overall integrity of the run forces the audience to interpret the unstressed prefix as a substitute for the "missing" inflectional syllable in an Sx/S pattern. In Czech verse, iambic meters and trochaic meters characteristically appear in separate runs or alternate within predictable stanzaic schemes (see Jakobson 1938). We shall see in section 5.3 that the Old English poet does impose a positional constraint on the most complex verse patterns, which are excluded from the second half-line.

2   Old English has a few enclitics, but these are affixed to small function words. A function word and accompanying enclitic, being too small to occupy a whole verse, will share a foot (see section 9.10 for a fairly clear case). A verse-final enclitic will thus form part of a foot rather than constituting a foot by itself.

3   This situation can arise only when a compound fills the whole verse pattern. When a compound shares the verse with another stressed word, rule (3b) confines the compound to a single foot, and its secondary constituent occupies an s position rather than an S position.

4   We shall see in section 6.2 that feet of the form Sxsx do occur, but only in clusters of "hypermetrical verses" carefully set apart from normal verses.

5 In section 10.2, I will argue that apparent examples of this pattern in *Beowulf* have been misinterpreted.

6 We will consider a few apparent exceptions to the four-position minimum in Chapter 10. These verses are regarded as corrupt by editors of standard editions.

7 A short stressed syllable occupying the first S position of the verse must be resolved except under the special conditions discussed in section 4.8 below.

8 According to my count, heavy "expanded D" verses with the patterns Sx/Ssx and Sx/Sxs occur only about one-fourth as often as do type D verses with the patterns S/Ssx or S/Sxs.

9 One apparent exception may be otherwise explained (see section 1.7, note 20).

10 A rule applies crucially to any verse that exhibits the features regulated by the rule. Rules (2) and (3) apply crucially to every verse. A rule such as (13a), however, does not always apply crucially (e.g. when the verse has no short foot).

NOTES TO CHAPTER 3

1 The OED defines *anacrusis* as "a syllable at the beginning of the verse before the just rhythm." In Old English metrics, the term designates one or more extrametrical syllables occurring verse-initially in type A1, A2, or D. The theory proposed here also allows for extrametrical syllables before the "light foot" of a type B or C verse; but I do not use the term *anacrusis* for such syllables.

2 Assuming that types B and C are divided according to the principles advocated here. In Sievers's theory, the first alliterating syllable of a type B or C verse is assigned to the first foot rather than to the second foot.

3 The Ss foot is somewhat less strongly associated with second position than are the long heavy feet Ssx, Sxs and Sxxs (see section 5.4.2). Yet the *Beowulf* poet avoids anacrusis before Ss/Sx patterns with perfect consistency. The apparent absence of long patterns such as Ss/Ssx, Ss/Sxx, Ss/Sxs, and Ss/Sxxs provides additional evidence that the Ss foot causes special complexity when it appears in first position (cf. section 1.7, note 20).

4 Cf. OEG, sections 87–8. The secondary constituents of compound neologisms are discussed in section 8.5 below.

5 Similar patterns do sometimes occur, but only in clusters of hypermetrical verses (cf. *Judith* 342b). Accordingly, we can state that there are no *normal* verses with the pattern (xx)Ssx/S. The hypermetrical verses in question seem to require two verse-initial unstressed syl-

lables rather than one (cf. section 6.4 below). If so, verses like (16) would be unacceptable under any conditions.

6 Note that Sx/Sx is the normative pattern, and therefore maximally tolerant of variation. The audience has a strong initial predisposition to posit the normative pattern, and would not easily be discouraged from doing so. Though acceptable, verses like (18a) are of course quite complex, and do not often occur.

7 We shall see in section 6.4 that this practice also helps establish a distinct boundary between normal verses and hypermetrical verses.

8 Cf. 438a, 1698a.

9 Cf. 473a, 1724b, 1941a, 2093a.

10 These emendations have been rejected by editors of standard editions (see e.g. Klaeber 1950, p. 278, I.c.).

11 There are no clear cases of anacrusis in b-verses with the pattern S/Sxx. Most editors emend the MS reading of verse 9b, *þara ymbsittendra,* to *ymbsittendra* on syntactic grounds. Dobbie (1953, 113–14) attempts to defend the MS reading, but the example of *ðāra he* cites as a parallel, being stressed and postposed, cannot qualify as a definite article.

12 The complexity associated with anacrusis is especially evident in the b-verse, where complexity of all types is avoided (cf. section 5.3). Here, moreover, there is a special danger of confusion between anacrusis and the "light feet" of hypermetrical verses (discussed in section 6.4).

NOTES TO CHAPTER 4

1 Recent work on child language acquisition provides evidence that the child learns rules in preference to memorizing isolated forms. For a convenient introduction to the subject, see Lightfoot (1982, 15–36, 172–84).

2 Cf. 528b.

3 Cf. 271a, 359a, 1680b, 1883a, 2736a.

4 Cf. 112b, 386b, 629b, 2034b, 2054b.

5 Cf. 820a, 1180a.

6 Cf. 3097b.

7 Recall that the "long diphthongs" spelled *ēa, ēo, īe, īo* are normally interpreted as equivalent to single long vowels (OEG, sections 37–9).

8 The rule may have been disregarded only in assessment of metricality. Poets do not necessarily attempt to reflect archaic metrical values in their pronunciation (see Kiparsky 1968, 177).

9 Cf. 1079a, 1440a, 1676a, 2742a.

10 Cf. 1187a, 1613a, 1681a, 1918a.

11 Cf. 1198a.

12 In Chomsky and Halle (1968, 187–8), for example, the authors posit for Modern English a synchronic rule of vowel shift and associated underlying forms resembling pronunciations of the late medieval period.

13 Note that the possibility of alternative interpretations arises only with respect to matching of linguistic material, not with respect to generation of foot patterns, which expresses an idealizing tendency. All resolvable sequences *generate* a single metrical position whether they have primary or secondary stress on the short vowel (cf. section 1.3).

14 Cf. 2912b.

15 Cf. 845a, 954a, 1828b.

16 Cf. 459a, 779a, 1514a, 1728a, 2048a.

17 Resolution may also be optional in verses with the pattern x/Sxx, and the rule is formulated to allow for that possibility. Crucial cases are hard to find because this pattern typically employs extrametrical words to signal the presence of the light foot. Most apparent examples of x/Sxx without resolution can therefore be interpreted as instances of xx/Sx with resolution. If we can accept the manuscript reading, *Beowulf* 1026a, *for scotenum,* would represent the crucial case (see Dobbie 1953, 168).

NOTES TO CHAPTER 5

1 It is obvious, however, that the usefulness of a pattern may have a significant effect on its relative frequency. The foot pattern Sxs, for example, is more complex than the pattern Ssx from a purely metrical point of view, and we might therefore expect Sxs to occur much less often. However, Sxs provides a convenient location for word groups in which the first constituent has an overt inflectional ending and the second constituent lacks such an ending. The half-line *þæt is / Hrǣdlan lāf* (454b) shows a genitive-noun construction with normal word order occupying an Sxs foot. One must employ unusual word order to place such constructions within a foot of the form Ssx. Heavy verses like *gesēon / sunu Hrǣdles* (1485a), in which the complexity associated with three stressed words is aggravated by complex syntax, occur very seldom in the poetic corpus. The concept of "usefulness" is discussed further in section 10.5.

2 The exact counts of particular verse patterns required to justify Sievers's assignment of "subtypes" to "basic types" will always be open to question. Here I attribute significance only to discrepancies that would be revealed by any reasonable counting procedure.

3 If feet derive from words, deviation with respect to any significant feature of word structure can obscure an underlying pattern. Principle I leads us to *expect* several different sources of complexity.

4 Compounds are in general less "word-like" than are simplexes (see section 1.1.2).

5 E.g. those variants of the x/Sxx pattern with a weak verbal preterite like *tryddode* in the second foot. I assume that the syntactically problematic *egsode eorl* (6a), with a weak preterite in the first foot and a monosyllabic word in the second foot, results from scribal error (see Dobbie 1953, 113).

6 My generous count accepted as examples of the x/Sxx pattern such half-lines as 3a, 64a, 139a, 144a, and 257a. The proportion of x/Sxx to x/Ssx remained less than 1:4 in the first half-line and less than 1:15 in the second half-line. The relatively lower frequency in the second half-line is a good indication of complexity (see section 5.3).

7 The pattern Sxx corresponds to lexicalized compounds and to forms of "weak verbs" derived from other parts of speech. Although forms like *tryddode* have no internal word boundaries, their morphemic structure is more complex than that of underived forms.

8 Poets in many different traditions restrict complexity at the end of a metrical domain. This preference for metrical closure may be in some sense universal (see Hayes 1983, 373).

9 I regard as "expanded" verses only those with a trochaic word occupying the first foot. In verses like *Hēold / (on) hēahgesceap* (3084a), one can exclude an extrametrical word from consideration to obtain an S/Sxs pattern with four positions.

10 We shall see in section 6.4 that hypermetrical b-verses usually resemble normal type A1 verses with two or more syllables in anacrusis. If the audience were used to seeing the sequence xxSx as a complete b-verse, there would be a false sense of closure after the xxSx portion of the hypermetrical verse.

11 Like (30b) are 845a, 954a, and 1828b. I found over fifty verses like (31), not counting those like 771a, which can be analyzed as x/Ssx (cf. PR2 (26)).

12 The patterns Sx/Ss and Ss/Sx both occur well over a hundred times in *Beowulf*. There are less than thiry occurrences of xx/Ss in the poem.

13 The others are 2007b, 2334b, 2959b, 2969b, and 3081b.

14 Verse 1261b, *siþðan camp wearð*, looks like such a variant, but it makes no sense in context. The usual emendation, *siþðan Cāin wearð*, is of doubtful value as evidence for a pattern not attested elsewhere in the poem.

15 Two non-proclitic function words in verse-initial position usually

signal the presence of an x foot, and would tend in general to be so interpreted.

NOTES TO CHAPTER 6

1   I regard as hypermetrical clusters verses 1163a-6b, 1167b-9b, 1705a-7b, 2995a-6b.
2   The same disproportion is evident in poems with a richer sample of hypermetrical patterns. In the first twenty lines of *Judith*, for example, one can find seven hypermetrical verses with large embedded compounds. I set aside the question of whether free-standing normal verses and corresponding embedded verses would have had the same rhythmical interpretation during performance.
3   Exclusion of the type A3 pattern xx/Sx from the second half-line prevents a false sense of closure in hypermetrical verses like (40). Cf. section 5.3.

NOTES TO CHAPTER 7

1   Like other metrists, I sometimes refer to verses that alliterate for example "on e-." This language merely serves to pick out an alliterating syllable from other syllables in a printed half-line, and should not be taken to imply that the identity requirement applies to vowels.
2   In Gothic, the labiovelar spelled ƕ also alliterates as a single constituent. The failure of OE *hw-* to alliterate as a single constituent shows that it has been reanalyzed as a biphonemic cluster (Kuryłowicz 1970, 15).
3   Kiparsky (1968, 170–1) argues that the "zero consonant" is not in fact a segment but a somewhat more abstract entity that figures in phonological rule systems.
4   A secondary set of equivalent syllables is occasionally found. Members of such a set can occupy positions where primary alliteration is forbidden. Although the secondary patterns do not "alliterate" in the usual sense, they probably had aesthetic significance. See Bennett (1980).
5   Half-lines with syntactically parallel constituents show an increased tendency toward double alliteration, which would indicate strong stress on the second constituent (see Sievers 1893, sections 23–5). Kuhn (1933, section 24) seems to ignore this evidence in arguing that the second of two parallel constituents was subordinated linguistically to the first. The theory of Maling (1971) is vulnerable to a similar objection. We need a concept of metrical subordination in any case to account for the absolute prohibition against alliteration

in the fourth foot of lines like (43d). Otherwise, we would have to say that the linguistic stress pattern of b-verses differed from that of a-verses with the same syntactic structure. It seems best to assume, with Kuryłowicz, that the metrical subordination responsible for alliterative patterns in the b-verse also affects the a-verse in certain ways.

6   We will discuss a few systematic exceptions in section 9.9.

7   Weak–strong branching occurs in Old English at the level of the phrase (e.g. when a function word is immediately followed by its governed constituent).

8   The Liberman–Prince theory involves a number of claims, some of them now quite controversial, that have nothing to do with this simple principle of compounding. The theory of alliteration advanced here does not of course stand or fall with such claims. Some linguists who reject certain features of Liberman–Prince (1977) nevertheless use tree structures to capture underlying relations of relative prominence (see e.g. Hayes 1983, 391). It seems possible, therefore, that the alliterative rules of Old English tell us something of general significance about underlying phonological representations (see section 7.6 for further discussion).

9   One finds this assumption e.g. in Halle and Keyser (1971, 95–6).

10   This variant is unattested in *Beowulf*. PPs does contain some verse patterns of the sort avoided consistently by the *Beowulf* poet, but in the absence of contrary evidence it seems reasonable to assume that (46a-b) represent the more widely acceptable pattern.

11   The right results seem to follow from the assumption that such weak syllables had reduced stress. In that case, they would generate x positions (see section 1.3). Syllables of reduced stress escape the constraints of (2a-c), and may occupy s or S positions in certain cases. If we accept the reading of 2152b suggested by Dobbie (1953, 227), the tertiary constituent *-hēafod-* in the triple compound *eaforhēafodsegn* corresponds to metrical sx in an Ssx/S pattern.

12   I give this subrule for clarity of exposition, but from a strictly theoretical point of view it is unnecessary. One can assume that alliteration is optional wherever not specifically required or forbidden.

13   Kuryłowicz (1970, 7) argues that the integrity of the Greek hexameter also results from application of word-level rules to word groups.

14   The others: 178a, 187a, 324a, 707a, 792a, 840a, 851a, 885a, 921a, 1146a, 1149a, 1704a, 2560a, 2652a, 2946a, 3150a. It is interesting to note that verses like *lēoflīc īren* (1809a) do not appear in the second half-line. If the absence of such b-verses is not accidental, it implies that the poet regarded the alliteration on *-līc / -lic-* as significant. In that case, we could add *lēoflīc lind-wiga* (2603a) and *lāðlicu*

lāc (1584a) to the list of verses with three alliterating syllables (cf. (57a-d)).

15 The others: 147a, 517a, 545a, 1395a, 2313a, 2650b, 2987a.

16 Clear cases are 168a, 219a, 484a, 1059a, 1496a, 1504a, 1599a, 1652a, 1877a, 1995a, 2101a, 2122a, 2258a, 2376a, 2389a, 2466a, 2699a, 2770a, 3174a. Doubtful cases: 506a, 1836a, 2437a (cf. OEG, 34 n. 4).

17 Clear cases are 193a, 330a, 485a, 608a, 1698a, 1719a, 1881a.

18 Hayes's article includes a critique of attempts by Prince (1983) and Selkirk (1984) to do away with trees entirely.

NOTES TO CHAPTER 8

1 Cf. 2509a, 2638a.

2 Cf. 496a, 1904a, 2638a.

3 Cf. 625a, 1274a, 2422a.

4 Cf. 1904b, 2156b, 2246b, 2469b, 2610b, 2662b, 2853b.

5 Cf. 478b, 583b, 2600b.

6 Cf. 496b, 515b, 892b, 1132b.

7 Cf. 494b, 1214b, 1520b, 3118b.

8 Cf. 210a.

9 *Beowulf* 1679a, with reference to an ancient sword; *Andreas* 1235a, with reference to a flagged street. The distinction in *Andreas* between *enta ǣrgeweorc* and *eald entageweorc* (1495a) seems identical to that observed in *Beowulf.*

10 The convenient terms *combinative* and *base* are adopted from Spamer (1977).

11 The typical kenning is an implied proportion with two terms concealed. Thus *hron-rād* is equivalent to a riddle of the form "a whale is to X as Y is to a road." Filling the blanks in an appropriate way, we obtain "a whale is to THE SEA as a man is to a road." The tradition supplies stereotyped contexts within which the proportion can be solved. Many kennings involve analogies between sea and land, for example.

12 Although *beer mug* is spelled "open," its secondary constituent has of course undergone subordination, and it must be regarded as a compound word. In the OED, a desire to find the earliest attestation of each word sometimes results in a misreading of poetic compounds. It is surely wrong to connect the *ealo-benc* of *Beowulf,* which doubled as a bed, with the *ale-bench* used within or outside an ale-house hundreds of years afterwards. The later term *ale-bench* does in fact refer to a piece of furniture reserved for drinking.

13 The name *Bēowulf* may be an old kenning with the meaning "Bee-

Wolf" (i.e., "bear"). The bear steals honey from the bee as the wolf
steals sheep from the herdsman. See Klaeber (1950, xxviii).

14 Duncan (1984) also claims that poetic compounds count as two
words. I have not reproduced his arguments here, and I hope that
they will soon appear in print.

15 One other apparent exception is explained below (example (101),
section 10.2).

16 The compound *mægen-hrēð* can be translated literally as "troop-
glory," and there is evidence that a meaning "glory-troop" would
also be possible. In 2795a, the familiar poetic compound *wuldur-
cyning* "glory-king" appears; in 665b, we find the unusual formation
kyning-wuldor, apparently with similar meaning. If *kyning-wuldor*
can refer to a glorious king, *mægen-hrēð* can refer to a glorious
troop. In that case, 445a can be interpreted to mean "glorious troop
of men," which fits the context perfectly well.

NOTES TO CHAPTER 9

1 In a half-line like *drēam gehȳrde* (88b), for example, the root syllable
of *-hȳrde* probably had a relative prominence like that of the subordinated root syllable *-geard-* in the whole-verse compound *middangeardes* (504b, 751b). Subordination of *-hȳrde* would of course have
taken place at the level of the phrase or sentence, while that of
-geard- would have taken place at the level of the word. Yet the same
relative prominence relations could result in both half-lines.

2 Examples of the xx//Sx/S pattern with double alliteration: 403a,
518a, 576a, 983a, 1115a, 1148a, 1405a, 1764a, 1950a, 2015a,
2052a, 2060a, 3005a, 3117a.

3 Lewis (1973) rightly objects to the notion that alliteration on the
verb in verses like (83a) was accidental. Cf. Bliss (1958, section 15).

4 Here *sceal* is not proclitic, being split from its governed infinitive
bescūfan by the interposed prepositional phrase *þurh slīðne nīð.* We
encounter the same type of situation in the very similar verse 186b.

5 Note that (3b) applies only to stressed syllables located within feet.
When a word with reduced stress like *nū* occupies an extrametrical
position, it need not obey constraints on bracketing. The same reasoning applies with respect to *wēold* in (86c).

6 Cf. 1743b, 2170b.

7 Enclitic words do not receive clause-final stress. In American English
constructions like *He couldn't stop it,* for example, *it* often has the
schwa vowel indicating reduction to zero stress. Note also the clause-
final contraction of *not* in e.g. *I tried to do it, but I couldn't.*

8 The alliterative option in the first foot would be especially useful

when metrical or syntactic constraints made it difficult to place a colorful verb in emphatic position at the end of the verse.

1 The lack of a macron on *-a* in *gēna* presupposes that the two words formed a lexicalized compound. According to Campbell (OEG, section 356), such lexicalization would have taken place relatively late.

2 Cf. *Azarias* 112a, *ā forð ēce* "ever henceforth eternally."

3 Cf. 186b.

4 Cf. 1792b, 2420b, 2721b.

5 A *fela* plus adjective structure alliterates on *fela* in *Beowulf* 27a, 1637a, 1888b; *Wife's Lament* 26a; *Maxims I* 75b; *Azarias* 140b, 156a; *Metrical Charm* 2, 36b; *Riddle* 12, 7a. Similar examples in which alliteration on *fela* is very probable are *Maxims I* 147a; *Rune Poem* 5a; *Beowulf* 2106a, 2950a; *Order of the World* 3a.

6 The number of apparent violations is surprisingly small for such a corrupt text. I found only two (359b, 410a). It would be unreasonable to suppose that there were four atypical violations of (50), two of which just happened to involve *swīðe*. Non-alliterating *swīðe* also appears before a governed adjective in *Judgment Day II* 193a and in *Lord's Prayer II* 19a (where the adjective is used adverbially). *Judgment Day II* exhibits a number of metrical irregularities, especially in verses with end-rhyme, but in the rhymeless verses there are few violations of the kind in question here. The meter of *Lord's Prayer II* is quite regular, though one would have expected alliteration on *twā* in line 20a. It seems clear, in any case, that *swīðe* plus adjective constructions have a metrical distribution unlike that of compounds.

7 For discussion of relations between the manuscript and the transcripts, see Zupitza-Davis (pp. v-xxi) and Dobbie (1953, xx-xxiv).

8 I exclude as unreadable verses 240b, 722b, 723b, 747b, 2001a, 2002a, 2007a, 2009a, 2019a, 2146b, 2212a, 2215b, 2216b, 2217a-b, 2219b, 2220a, 2223b, 2225a, 2226b-2231a, 2253a, 2275a, 2276a, 2299a, 2361b, 2678a, 2714b, 3014a, 3041a, 3150b-3155a, 3157a, 3158a, 3168b, 3171a, 3177b, 3179a.

9 Lines 9, 62, 389, 403, 414, 457, 954, 1129, 1329, 1372, 1803, 1875, 1889, 1926, 2251, 2792, 2941, 3000, 3086, 3101, 3136.

10 Lines 149, 586, 965, 1073, 1981, 2139, 2525.

11 Verses 574b, 2916b.

12 Dobbie (1953, 245) notes a similar formation *wīg-blāc* "battle-bright" in *Exodus* 204a. The meaning of *hilde-blāc* would probably be "battle-bright" rather than "battle-pale," with reference to the king's armor rather than to his bloodless complexion. Mention of a

fallen nobleman's splendid equipment, which will be subject to plunder by adversaries, is an almost obligatory feature of Old English battle narratives (cf. *Maldon* 159a-68a).

13 On the basis of an ultraviolet photograph, Pope (1942, 350) argued that the manuscript originally did read *7cyning*. However, subsequent examination of the manuscript seems to indicate that *kyning* was the reading after all (see Zupitza-Davis, p. xii). The manuscript is very badly faded here.

14 Cable (1974, 37–43) provides a careful comparison of poetry to prose in his discussion of type A with anacrusis. Here the focus of investigation is relatively narrow, and a small corpus of prose "half-lines" is sufficient to make the point.

15 Verse units 2b, 120b, 121b, 257b.

16 I.e., syllables with primary stress or unreduced secondary stress.

17 Cf. verse units 157a, 287a.

18 Cf. 221b.

19 Cf. 237a.

20 Cf. 172b, 191a, 274a.

21 Cf. 59a, 113a, 118a, 168a, 189a, 204a.

22 Cf. 1b, 43b, 54a, 151b, 166a, 176a, 235b, 283a.

23 In order to avoid problems of ambiguity, I consider only those verse units with alliterating syllables placed in the proper locations for type B or C.

WORKS CITED

Amos, A. (1980). *Linguistic Means of Determining the Dates of Old English Literary Texts.* Cambridge, Massachusetts: Medieval Academy of America.

ASPR: see Krapp and Dobbie (1931–53).

Bauer, L. (1983). *English Word-formation.* Cambridge, London, New York, New Rochelle, Melbourne, and Sydney: Cambridge University Press.

Behaghel, O. (1897). *Die Syntax des Heliand.* Vienna and Prague: F. Tempsky; Leipzig: G. Freytag.

—— (1965). *Heliand und Genesis.* 8th ed. revised by W. Mitzka. Tübingen: Max Niemeyer [cited as Behaghel-Mitzka].

Bennett, H. (1980). Extra Alliteration as a Stylistic Device in Beowulf. Doctoral dissertation, Brown University.

Bessinger, J., Jr., and S. J. Kahrl, eds. (1968). *Essential Articles for the Study of Old English Poetry.* Hamden, Connecticut: Archon Books.

Bliss, A. J. (1958). *The Metre of Beowulf.* Oxford: Basil Blackwell.

——(1972). "The Origin and Structure of the Old English Hypermetric Line." *Notes and Queries* 19, 242–8.

Borroff, M. (1962). *Sir Gawain and the Green Knight: A Stylistic and Metrical Study.* New Haven and London: Yale University Press.

Bosworth, J., and T. N. Toller (1898). *An Anglo-Saxon Dictionary; Supplement,* by T. N. Toller (1921); *Enlarged Addenda and Corrigenda,* by A. Campbell (1972). London: Oxford University Press [cited as Bosworth-Toller].

Brodeur, A. G. (1959). *The Art of Beowulf.* Berkeley and Los Angeles: University of California Press.

Cable, T. (1974). *The Meter and Melody of Beowulf.* Urbana, Chicago, and London: University of Illinois Press.

Campbell, A. (1959). *Old English Grammar.* Oxford: Oxford University Press [cited as OEG].

—— (1972): see Bosworth and Toller (1898).

Works Cited

Cassidy, F., and R. Ringler (1971). *Bright's Old English Grammar and Reader,* 3rd. ed. [second corrected printing]. New York: Holt, Rinehart and Winston.

Chambers, R. W. (1967). *Beowulf: An Introduction,* 3rd. ed. with a supplement by C. L. Wrenn. Cambridge: Cambridge University Press.

Chomsky, N. (1968). *Language and Mind.* New York: Harcourt, Brace and World.

Chomsky, N., and M. Halle (1968). *The Sound Pattern of English.* New York: Harper and Row.

Clark Hall, J. R., and H. D. Meritt (1969). *A Concise Anglo-Saxon Dictionary.* Cambridge: Cambridge University Press.

Creed, R. P. (1966). "A New Approach to the Rhythm of *Beowulf.*" *PMLA* 81, 23–33.

Daunt, M. (1947). "Old English verse and English speech rhythm." *Transactions of the Philological Society* (for 1946), 56–72; cited from rpt. in Bessinger and Kahrl, eds. (1968), pp. 289–304.

Dobbie, E. V. K. (1953). *Beowulf and Judith* [vol. 4 of Krapp and Dobbie (1931–53)].

Duncan, E. (1984). Stress, Meter, and Alliteration in Old English Poetry. Doctoral dissertation, University of Texas, Austin.

Halle, M., and S. J. Keyser (1966). "Chaucer and the Study of Prosody." *College English* 28, 187–219.

——— (1971). *English Stress: Its Form, Its Growth, and Its Role in Verse.* New York: Harper and Row.

Hayes, B. (1983). "A Grid-based Theory of English Meter." *Linguistic Inquiry* 14, 357–93.

——— (1984). "The Phonology of Rhythm in English." *Linguistic Inquiry* 15, 33–74.

Jakobson, R. (1938). "K popsiu Máchova verše," in J. Mukařovský, ed., *Torso a tajemství Máchova díla,* Borovy, Prague, pp. 207–78; cited from the English translation, "Toward a Description of Mácha's Verse," by P. and W. Steiner, in Jakobson (1979), 433–85.

——— (1963). "On the So-Called Vowel Alliteration in Germanic Verse." *Zeitschrift für Phonetik, Sprachwissenschaft und Kommunikationsforschung* 16, 85–92; cited from Jakobson (1979), 189–97.

——— (1979). *Selected Writings, vol. 5.* The Hague: Mouton.

Jespersen, O. (1924). *The Philosophy of Grammar.* London: George Allen and Unwin.

Keyser, S. J. (1969). "Old English Prosody." *College English* 30, 331–56.

Kiparsky, P. (1968). "Metrics and Morphophonemics in the Kalevala," in D. C. Freeman, ed., *Linguistics and Literary Style.* New York: Holt, Rinehart and Winston.

—— (1972). "Metrics and Morphophonemics in the Rigveda," in M. Brame, ed., *Contributions to Generative Phonology*. Austin, Texas: University of Texas Press.

—— (1977). "The Rhythmic Structure of English Verse." *Linguistic Inquiry* 8, 189–247.

—— (1982). "From Cyclic Phonology to Lexical Phonology," in Hulst, H., and N. Smith, eds., *The Structure of Phonological Representations, Part I*. Dordrecht, Holland and Cinnaminson, New Jersey: Foris Publications.

Kiparsky, P., and W. O'Neil (1976). "The Phonology of Old English Inflections." *Linguistic Inquiry* 7, 527–57.

Klaeber, F. (1950). *Beowulf and the Fight at Finnsburg*, 3rd. ed. Boston: D. C. Heath.

Krapp, G. P., and E. V. K. Dobbie (1931–53). *The Anglo-Saxon Poetic Records*, 6 vols. New York: Columbia University Press [cited as ASPR].

Kuhn, H. (1933). "Zur Wortstellung und -betonung im Altgermanischen." *Beiträge zur Geschichte der deutschen Sprache und Literatur* 57, 1–109.

Kuryłowicz, J. (1970). *Die sprachlichen Grundlagen der altgermanischen Metrik*. Innsbruck: Institut für vergleichende Sprachwissenschaft.

—— (1975). *Metrik und Sprachgeschichte* [Polska Akademia Nauk, Warsaw; Komitet Językoznawstwa; Prace językoznawcze 83]. Wrocław: Zakład Narodowy imienia Ossolińskich.

Lehmann, R. P. M. (1975). "Broken Cadences in *Beowulf*." *English Studies* 56, 1–13.

Lehmann, W. P. (1968). "Post-Consonantal *l m n r* and Metrical Practice in *Beowulf*," in A. H. Orrick, ed., *Nordica et Anglica: Studies in Honor of Stefán Einarsson*, Janua Linguarum, Series Maior 22. The Hague: Mouton.

Lewis, R. A. (1973). "Alliteration and Old English Metre." *Medium Ævum* 42, 119–30.

Liberman, M., and A. Prince (1977). "On Stress and Linguistic Rhythm." *Linguistic Inquiry* 8, 249–336.

Lightfoot, D. (1982). *The Language Lottery: Toward a Biology of Grammars*. Cambridge, Massachusetts and London, England: MIT Press.

Lord, A. (1960). *The Singer of Tales*. Cambridge, Massachusetts: Harvard University Press.

Lowenstamm, J. (1981). "On the Maximal Cluster Approach to Syllable Structure." *Linguistic Inquiry* 12, 575–604.

Magoun, F. P. (1953). "Oral-Formulaic Character of Anglo-Saxon Narrative Poetry." *Speculum* 28, 446–67.

Maling, J. (1971). "Sentence Stress in Old English." *Linguistic Inquiry* 11, 379–99.

Works Cited

Meid, W. (1967). *Wortbildungslehre*, vol. 3 of H. Krahe and W. Meid, *Germanische Sprachwissenschaft*. Berlin: Walter de Gruyter.

Mitchell, B. (1968). *A Guide to Old English*. Oxford: Basil Blackwell.

Murphy, G. (1961). *Early Irish Metrics*. Dublin: Royal Irish Academy.

Neckel, G. and H. Kuhn (1962), eds. *Edda: die Lieder des Codex Regius nebst verwandten Denkmälern*. Heidelberg: Carl Winter.

OED: The Oxford English Dictionary.

OEG: see Campbell (1959).

Pope, J. C. (1942). *The Rhythm of Beowulf*. New Haven: Yale University Press.

—— (1967). *Homilies of Ælfric: A Supplementary Collection, Vol. I* [Early English Text Society No. 259]. London and New York: Oxford University Press.

Prince, A. (1983). "Relating to the Grid." *Linguistic Inquiry* 14, 19–100.

Robinson, F. (1962). Variation: A Study in the Diction of Beowulf. Doctoral dissertation, University of North Carolina.

Russom, G. (1978). "Artful Avoidance of the Useful Phrase in *Beowulf, The Battle of Maldon,* and *Fates of the Apostles.*" *Studies in Philology* 75, 371–90.

—— (1984). "Old English Meter." Paper delivered at the Nineteenth International Congress on Medieval Studies, Medieval Institute, Western Michigan University, Kalamazoo, May 11.

Selkirk, E. (1984). *Phonology and Syntax: The Relation between Sound and Structure*. Cambridge, Massachusetts: MIT Press.

Sievers, E. (1885). "Zur Rhythmik des germanischen Alliterationsverses." *Beiträge zur Geschichte der deutschen Sprache und Literatur* 10, 209–314, 451–545.

—— (1893). *Altgermanische Metrik*. Halle: Max Niemeyer.

Sisam, K. (1953). *Studies in the History of Old English Literature*. Oxford: Clarendon Press.

Spamer, J. B. (1977). The Kenning and Kend Heiti: A Contrastive Study of Periphrasis in Two Germanic Poetic Traditions. Doctoral dissertation, Brown University.

Travis, J. (1973). *Early Celtic Versecraft*. Ithaca, New York: Cornell University Press.

Wrenn, C. L., and W. F. Bolton (1973). *Beowulf, with the Finnesburg Fragment*. New York: St. Martin's Press.

Zupitza, J. (1959). *Beowulf: Reproduced in Facsimile from the Unique Manuscript, British Museum Ms. Cotton Vitellius A. xv,* 2nd. ed. revised by N. Davis [Early English Text Society No. 245]. London: Oxford University Press [cited as Zupitza-Davis].

BEOWULF VERSES OF SPECIAL INTEREST

Some of the verses listed below are unmetrical; others are unusual or complex. References are to page numbers in this volume.

Beowulf Verses of Special Interest

INDEX

Items are not listed below if they appear in the table of contents or in "Beowulf Verses of Special Interest."

Index